The Words of Ahmose:

The Magic of Perfect Loving

by

Elijah Mickel, MSW, MA, DSW, CRT

DORRANCE
PUBLISHING CO
EST. 1920
PITTSBURGH, PENNSYLVANIA 15238

Dorrance Publishing Co
585 Alpha Drive
Suite 103
Pittsburgh, PA 15238
Visit our website at *www.dorrancebookstore.com*

ISBN: 979-8-88729-166-6
eISBN: 979-8-88729-666-1

TABLE OF CONTENTS

Acknowledgment	vii
Preface	ix
Introduction	xi
Born of the Moon (Ahmose)	1
Miracle (IJAH)	2
Magic (Space) Box	4
The Magic Place	5
Trust Weus	6
Trust	7
Hope Beyond the Rope	8
Love Hard	9
Loss	10
I Await the Dawn	12
Dawn and Sunrise	15
Sweet Sweet Lips	16
New Dawn	17
NWAD	19
The Warriors Blood	20
Malaika	23
Angel on Earth	25
Happy Day Sadly	27
Heavenly Thine	28
I Dream of Heaven	29
Gates of Heaven	30
Rivers of Gold	32
Land of Gold	34
Our Gold Mine	37
African Mine	38
The Weeping Tree	39
Needing Mo	41
If You Left	42

To Kiss Your Lips	43
Wind and Spirit	45
Collmine	46
I Feel the	47
More	48
On the Path	49
Caring Sounds	50
Love to	51
Why	52
Okra's Spoon	53
Now is Our Time	54
Kemet Lovers	56
I Think of My Baby	57
Arms of Love	58
Dreams of Us	59
Ship on the Ocean	60
Can't Wait	61
Without Struggle	62
The Letter	63
Tonight	64
Lovers Well Met	65
Heart Sings	66
My Baby (Mine)	67
Infinity	69
Excuse	70
Maybe	71
Into the Deep	72
Vegan Coffee	74
Afternoon Tea	75
Killing Roses	76
Story of the Reed	77
Saluting the Sun	79
The Bowl Sings to Thee	81
House of Time	83
Period of Time	85

Transition	86
Waterway	87
Burnt People Land	90
Butterfly	91
Weeding and Seeding	93
Cutting Branches	95
Step on Evil	96
I Don't Know	98
Voices I Hear	101
Resarection	102
Herd	103
On the Path	104
First Great	105
Burning Embers of Hate	106
One Path	107
Closing Eyes	108
Spirit Hello	109
Easy Days	110
Queen in Green	111
Green Car	113
In the Air	114
End of Beginning	115
Shadow	116
Only One	117
Fading Dreams	118
Insight	119
Shopping	120
First and Last	121
Why He Came	122
Waiting	123
Clouds	124
Written by C. Mickel	125
Black Body Expert	126
Accepted Control	127
Possible	128

Ancestors 129

Ignorance 130

Wisdom 131

Husband or wife 132

Asking why 133

Altars 134

Cause/Effect 135

Soul Sustains 136

Today 137

BRTHDY 138

These Loving Hands 139

Vessel of Loving 140

George to George 141

Eve 142

Soap 143

Significant Other 144

Constant Presence 145

Touch of Death 146

I Am So Tired 147

Dark 148

Hail to the King 149

Mask 150

It's Raining 151

Pleasure Without Joy 152

I Met You 153

What I Thought 154

WORDS OF COLLEEN

Eternities Corridor 155

Thankful 156

Thank You 157

Bended Knees 158

Quietly We Wait 159

Simply Meant to Be 160

EPILOGUE 161

ACKNOWLEDGMENT

These poems serve a number of purposes for many people, but for me, they were therapy in the midst of a storm. I therefore acknowledge the value of *The Words of Ahmose*. To generations of the past, present, and future, they open the way. We cannot move forward without acknowledging the struggles of our past. We, present generation, cannot heal from the past without looking at the transformations occurring in the present. We cannot expect a better future if we are holding on to yesterday. So, accept your past with no regrets, live in the present with extreme confidence, and face the future without fear. The world is YOURS.

Kamryn Mickel, BSW
Founder - The Ladies Room

PREFACE

The Words of Ahmose began with born of the moon. This leads to a miracle found in magic from the magic place. There we trust weus, a place of trust. Next, we find hope beyond the rope where we love hard in spite of loss. Now I await the dawn, dawn, and sunrise bring the new dawn. There are sweet lips of NWAD based in the warrior's blood. Malaika is the angel on earth. Happy day, sadly she is heavenly thine. When I dream of heaven, taken to the gates of heaven. I find rivers of gold in the land of gold containing our gold mine, an African mine.

Where is the weeping tree. Ahmose words reflect needing Mo, if you left. Remembering to kiss your lips feeling the wind and spirit of Collmine. I feel the connection more when on the path I hear caring sounds of precious love to understand why when using okra's spoon. It reflects now is our time. Well met are Kemet lovers where I think of my baby in my arms of love. Here we dream of us as a ship on the ocean seeking now and can't wait for time without struggle. Herein receiving the letter written tonight expressing feelings as lovers well met where our heart sings of my baby (mine). Infinity is not an excuse, maybe into the deep drinking vegan coffee and afternoon tea. The killing of roses in the story of the need saluting the sun. The bowl sings to thee in the house of time for a period of time making the transition on the waterway leading to the burnt people land.

A butterfly weeding and seeding cutting branches building the step on evil which I don't know. Voices I hear leading to resarection-. There is a herd on the path one path first great. There are burning embers which result in hate to closing eyes. While the spirit hello leads to the easy days which find the Queen in green in a green car, in the air leading to the end of beginning.

There is a shadow, only one with fading dreams giving insight for shopping. The first and last understand. Why he came waiting in the clouds. This was written by C. Mickel, a black body expert. He accepted control as possible from the ancestors. Ignorance leads to wisdom with husband and wife asking why at the altars. There is a cause/effect the soil sustains today our BRTHDY. These loving hands are a vessel of love as George to George foretold. The eve is soap to the significant other whose constant presence obviates the touch of death for I am so tired in the dark. Hail to the king while wearing a mask. Although it's raining, there is pleasure without joy until I met you. Oh, what a thought. In the words of Colleen in eternities corridor, we are thankful as I thank you on bended knees. Simply meant to be as quietly we wait for Ahmose's words as thoughts of perfect love.

INTRODUCTION

Normally an introduction is used to prepare the reader for the text. I would like to use my pen to introduce you to the writer. Dr. Mickel (Ahmose Neb Pehte Ra) is that author. He has authored a number of books as well as articles. Two previous books of poetry (one I co-authored). Thus, this is the third book of poetry by him. These poems range from love and relationships to philosophical musing. It begins with magic and ends with a short poem by his grandson (my son), Inspired, I write the following to introduce the Words of Ahmose:

Literally literacy leads to legendary literary works of beauty intense emotions and cognitive content
But once content one rarely will flourish
At times not about the rhyme as long as one continues to cultivate minds
What is the purpose and why should they listen
Are you providing nourishment as the Sun what is the intention
See I signify dignified most times each line is a sense of pride sometimes I get a peace of mind
My tales and trails trials and fails
I share a piece of mines
So you aligned on your grind
Shouldn't be blind when its time
Don't cross that line cause it's all been defined
I value honesty integrity and truth some embellish as long as it's a message I get it
Tears fall from my eyes as rain fall from the sky
That's concrete beneath my feet
Stay on the side walk it ain't safe in these streets
Educated but never hesitated
The ink from my pen or lead from my pencil expresses
My fear is courage not one without the other
Anger and sadness always from the day I lost my brother

Christopher Jeremy Mickel

BORN OF THE MOON

Today, very day we celebrate him born of the moon
Moon rise is the reflection of the sun's power
Power to rise and unite the people's movement
Movement united to find the way to freedom
Freedom as he followed the lord's strength
Strength to prepare the way to overcome
Overcome those who would seek to dominate
Dominate the followers of the way straight
Straight is belief in balance, right and truth
Truth to self and to those we are committed
Committed to do what is right night to day
Day is the reflected light which brightens our life
Life that exists in the here and eternity
Eternity exists for those who the way believe
Believe not that there is nonexistence
Nonexistence comes into being through acceptance
Acceptance of limitations and defeat
Defeat occurs when one begins to doubt
Doubt the very power given to us
Us as the joining of the river of life born of the moon

MIRACLE (IJAH)

There is a miracle floating in the air
Reach up and grab it there

Each is entitled to have more than one
Some through their faith get some

To search is the way to find the unknown
That which is found is the way home

When there is little to no light
Miracles makes the dark bright

In the midst of a sought miracle of hope
Can be found existing the many ways to cope

Each day of life regardless of condition is a gift
The belief that it is better although relations may rift

The faith of those neglected
Receive even more than expected

The desire that can end all killing
Only if those with faith are willing

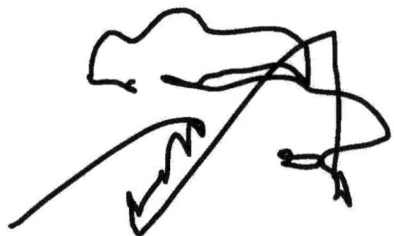

In the midst of a drought without rain
To find the end to dryness without pain

The belief of those who are neglected
A path to the dark way rejected

It is the impossible that you conceive
A happening that can be believed

Depending on that which is yet to be
Understanding that the invisible you can see

That although illness we may feel
The miracle contains words that heal

Every life that is saved
Road to eternity a soul paved

MAGIC (SPACE) BOX

This magic space lies within the dawn's light
When the sunrises it enters sweet delight
There is magic and I know where
It fills me with longing wishing to go there

I desire magic night and day
It fills me with more than I can say
There is a way to slide between walls
Hard within upon magic grass dew warmly falls

When inside magic, I came
This provides a way to provide same
Searched for magic all my life long
When found joy released with song

It can be found within the one
Know only when you come you are done
Wishing to be good at the use
Must be able to electrically release the juice

How good it makes me feel
Its use has the power which heals
This magic space lies within the dawn's light
When the sunrises it enters sweet delight

THE MAGIC PLACE

Only an angel guards the way
And keeps its entrance by her say
There is a magic place
It is a sacred space
It may be shrouded by lace
Approach it like flowers in a vase
To gain admittance make your case
Do not do so in haste
Take your time, slow your pace
To obtain it, do not race
Obtaining makes you an ace
You cannot force your way even with a mace
Once you leave it cannot be sealed as paste
Acquiring it gives just a taste
Here you can have joy on your face
When you enter, you find grace
Only an angel guards the base
And keeps its entrance by her say
There is a magic place
It is a sacred space

TRUST WEUS

In the word and construct where find concept weus
Weus must trust.
Without trust no us there
Trust is a must.
Trust power grows with the power of us.
This is a test that we will and must pass
Believe, love, trust.
It is a choice.
To choose to love, dream, notice, experience, feel.
Embrace love as weus loves love
Love enough to say I love you, eye trust you
Love enough to expect love in return
In the word and construct where find concept weus

TRUST

In our relationship forever we trust
We became in eternity a must

Today I waited for your call
Waiting did not hear from you at all

Tomorrow you said I wait
Saying be patient still too late

Until all we have turns to dust
Unlike metal our in loving never rust

Until dawn enters the sunrise
All truth is false and trusting lies

When the dew falls upon the grass
There is the revelation for both at last

In our relationship forever we trust
We became in eternity a must

HOPE BEYOND THE ROPE

This history includes lynching by the rope
Strangling with a noose choking a person without hope

The stars of the little Red Book
Denied their historical participation wherever you look

Now it is done within the law through a blue's gun
Assaulting a community putting African's on the run

Identify the enemy and its evil within
The treatment is not to be forgiven just a sin

United the oppressed can find a way
The hands of the oppressor to stay

Those of the community from whence the victim reside
Find a way day to day in union crying umoja to put fear aside

The truth acts as light to darkness end
A lie used to provide justification not to mend

It is the responsibility of those victimized
The truth of the victims to revitalize

Determined to take rope in own hands
Rise up with hope as the conscious Africans

LOVE HARD

Love live laugh
With you I love hard...
With you I live hard...
With you I laugh hard
With you I love Mo
With you I live Mo
With you I laugh Mo
With you is the joy of loving
With you is the joy of living
With you is the joy of laughing...
In you I love
In you I live
In you I laugh...
With us we love hard

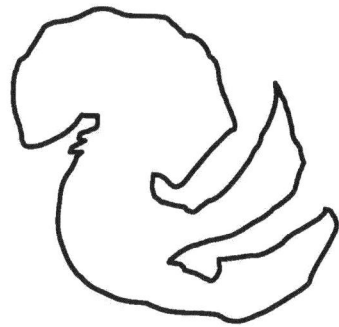

LOSS

The loss of those you wish to keep
Increased pain causes one to weep

What do you do when dealing with loss
How do you adjust to the emotional cost

The loss of those you wish to keep
Increased pain causes one to weep

On life's journey without you I lost my way
With you I was able to turn night to day

The loss of those you wish to keep
Increased pain causes one to weep

When I did not know the path correct
Under your guidance misery no regret

The loss of those you wish to keep
Increased pain causes one to weep

While nightly weeping I did endure
Through your presence joy is assured

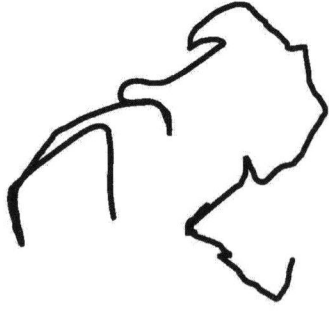

The loss of those you wish to keep
Increased pain causes one to weep

Although loved ones unable to protect
Unhappiness alone apart only to expect

The loss of those you wish to keep
Increased pain causes one to weep

To learn to disconnect from things
Decreases the comfort losing brings

The loss of those you wish to keep
Increased pain causes one to weep

Although the loved are visible present
The desire for interconnection is inconsistent

The loss of those you wish to keep
Increased pain causes one to weep

I AWAIT THE DAWN

The sunrise enters the dawn
Morning finds wet dew drops on the lawn

So long is the night
Time without you in sight

The sunrise enters the dawn
Morning finds wet dew drops on the lawn

A light breaks the day
Great is the morning on its way

The sunrise enters the dawn
Morning finds wet dew drops on the lawn

The dark gives way to day
Sunrise and dawn together lay

The sunrise enters the dawn
Morning finds wet dew drops on the lawn

There we find twice the light
Joined to reflect what is right

The sunrise enters the dawn
Morning finds wet dew drops on the lawn

From dusk to dawn waiting
A journey soon a pair mating

The sunrise enters the dawn
Morning finds wet dew drops on the lawn

The time between then and now
Joined sunrise and dawn showing how

The sunrise enters the dawn
Morning finds wet dew drops on the lawn

The sunrise plants a seed
The dawn receives this need

The sunrise enters the dawn
Morning finds wet dew drops on the lawn

Always within my thought
Constantly a picture of us sought

The sunrise enters the dawn
Morning finds wet dew drops on the lawn

I search for your sound
Integrating us joy is found

The sunrise enters the dawn
Morning finds wet dew drops on the lawn

Lead me to the place of us
There we find unity and trust

The sunrise enters the dawn
Morning finds wet dew drops on the lawn

DAWN AND SUNRISE

When the dawn peeks above the earth's rim
The sunrise then not far behind breaks the dim

The first harbinger of light
Busting forth making bright

No matter how dark the sky
It can be an explanation why

The dawn dips into your dreams
Sunrise burst forth walking unseen

Sunrise is the committed life complete
A cycle of day to night light replete

Dawn is the promise of light to come
Sunrise is the assurance of new day begun

Sunrise and dawn join together
A union of early and bright light ever

They rise through the trees
Find us thankful on our knees

When the dawn peeks above the earth's rim
The sunrise then not far behind breaks the dim

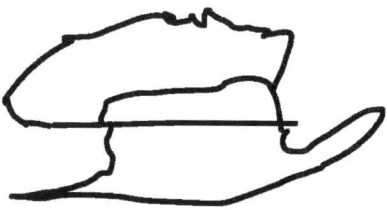

SWEET SWEET LIPS

All day and most of the night thinking of your sweet sweet lips
Driving out of my head hands can't seem to get a grip

There is a place I yearn to enter receiving a honey kiss
As I near the portal the passage where I can receive bliss

Can't stand another moment without bringing you near
Knowing in my life the only lack is not holding your dear

I think of you as my root with many branches a tree
That whatever you do will constantly satisfy me

It is when as waves they part or come together they pleased
Upon the edge or within the mist my total pleasure seized

Deep within where is developed the essence of life
You find a way to slice into my soul dividing like a knife

We reach out to envelope the total of our connection
Thus within the closeness of one to another no rejection

From the words that request connection is where begins the quips
Words that draw one in to taste the sweet sweet lips

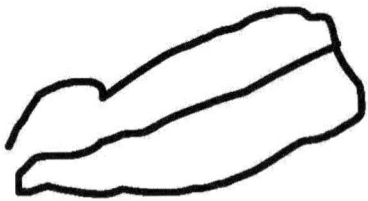

NEW DAWN

Each morning brings a new dawn
Followed by a rising of the sun warm

Often a night without both so cold
Awaiting the new day desiring you to hold

Gently feeling the new light
Bringing into existence my delight

The warmth of touching your skin
Feeling the heat of a glow within

This is a new day begun
Meeting my need done

Dawn I picture in each of my dreams
With the coming sun I know what it means

From the state of sleep to awake
In this journey one we make

Your presence takes me to the top
My beating heart seems to stop

Waiting for me you come
Joined in happiness sharing some

The dawn brings the sun which comes with a burst
Those who desire connection it satisfies their thirst

It brings forth such glee
Fulfills my desire within me

Greater is the need for your time
Allows all that is you to be mine

You as the wish fulfilled is real
Better than another satisfying meal

Tonight is the sum of another date set
You are each of my essential needs met

NWAD

NWAD is the way to all
Lights the morning standing tall
NWAD rises every day
As it brightens it leads the way
All wait for NWAD's sight
That time shinning bright
NWAD is the personification of life
When it appears connects like a wife
NWAD appears in the natural state
Always on time, never late

THE WARRIORS BLOOD

That we are of one (African) blood
Coursed and runs as warriors should
There is the blood that connected
No matter what others said it protected

The path is identified by the blood
A choice to follow because we could
Victory as we walked along the way
Assured by all we could do, feel, and say

That we are of one (African) blood
Coursed and runs as warriors should
There is the blood that connected
No matter what others said it protected

We are the ones of the blood
Whether from the suburbs or the hood
Together when each sighted
In our presence we delight

That we are of one (African) blood
Coursed and runs as warriors should
There is the blood that connected
No matter what others said it protected

As members of the spiritual blood
Survived combat at sea, sky and in mud
The strength to overcome oppression
Held together without succession

That we are of one (African) blood
Coursed and runs as warriors should
There is the blood that connected
No matter what others said it protected

Within the physical soul blood
There the chosen united stood
Some came to tear us apart
Did not understand connected heart

That we are of one (African) blood
Coursed and runs as warriors should
There is the blood that connected
No matter what others said it protected

Wherever they searched they found
There was seen a way to obtain the crown
That we are of many united nomes
Living and fighting for our homes

That we are of one (African) blood
Coursed and runs as warriors should
There is the blood that connected
No matter what others said it protected

Members join to form a tide of blood
Washes over opponents like a flood
Come together one body as they believe
Others choose to be separate and deceived

That we are of one (African) blood
Coursed and runs as warriors should
There is the blood that connected
No matter what others said it protected

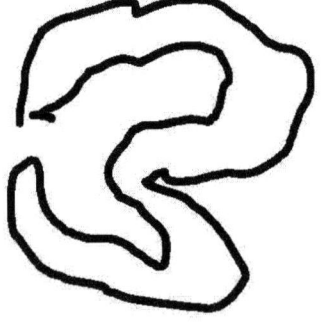

MALAIKA

For a lifetime I search for Malaika
Through fire and flood, calm and storm I sought her

Throughout my life for her I yearned
Met with many though they were returned

Seemed to be not whole incomplete
Although with some it was destiny for us to meet

The dawn is the essence of her beauty true
Interconnected with the sunrise morning dew

You are my angel fair
Unique of beauty with African hair

When the spirit speaks internal
It has a focus traveling to the eternal

In your presence refreshing waters flow
Thus you are present wherever we go

Spirit talking to my heart brings joy
Like a child, with a brand-new toy

Spiritual energy is pure communication
When both are connected with determination

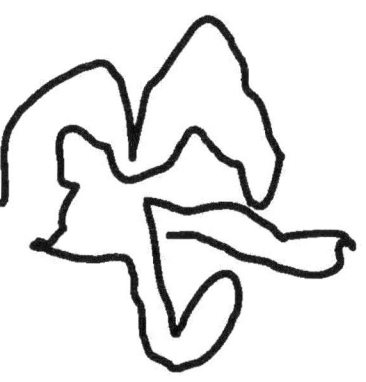

Therein lies the essence of us
Based upon this belief together we trust

The search for her began with first breath
Will continue until none is left

With her there is perfection
Which can be found in the connection

For a lifetime I search for Malaika
Through fire and flood, calm and storm I sought her

ANGEL ON EARTH

My angel came with magic to share
Choose to connect and be involved if you dare
Can happen if true all you choose to bare

There is a new angel on earth
Came to provide value increase worth

My angel came with magic to share
Choose to connect and be involved if you dare
Can happen if true all you choose to bare

My angel is the answer to prayers
A visible manifestation of creator cares

My angel came with magic to share
Choose to connect and be involved if you dare
Can happen if true all you choose to bare

Many looked for those with wings
Some understand this angel answers bring

My angel came with magic to share
Choose to connect and be involved if you dare
Can happen if true all you choose to bare

They came to problem solve
As an answer to prayers request resolve

My angel came with magic to share
Choose to connect and be involved if you dare

Can happen if true all you choose to bare

A messenger bringing the light
Receiving the way to end the night

My angel came with magic to share
Choose to connect and be involved if you dare
Can happen if true all you choose to bare

HAPPY DAY SADLY

It was a happy day
When you came my way

It was a sad occasion when you left
All that I had taken as a theft

It seemed to me being tossed
Bearing the trauma like a cross

Life like a light without a socket
Trying to reignite new feelings like a rocket

I should have known the feeling
Because my happiness had no ceiling

Each time we parted emotionally bereft
Seems I had the feeling of loss like death

HEAVENLY THINE

This property heavenly thine
Traveling golden streets in my mind
Through heavenly gates to thee find
Entering losing all that's mine
Feeling like having too much wine
When away each moment pine
Returning quickly so incline
When hungry there to dine
Finding way without map or sign
Searched all over without kind
Looked here and there not blind
Wishing to enter don't decline
Hoping to explore the whole nine
No need to alter or refine
This property heavenly thine

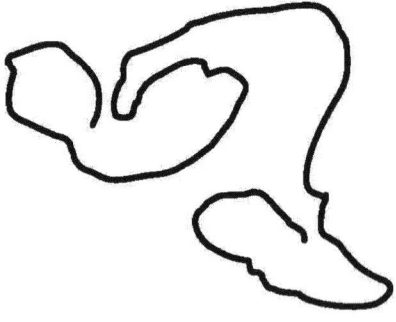

I DREAM OF HEAVEN

I dream of the day when I heaven enter
It is the focus of my life held at the center

O when the gates they do part
In I go yes quickly I dart

It seems to be a misty place
Though within I feel safe

This is the place of my dreams
It is as good to me as it seems

I enter alone traveling fast
Safe and secure home at last

As I enter I know it is magic's place
Surrounded held close in this space

As upon command exhale dawn to sun
Know that what I am given is fun

Today is the day following the way
It is where I wish to ever stay

My heart beats just strumming
Here I came, I yell I'm coming

GATES OF HEAVEN

It is here one taste the fruit of the tree
This is where one lives eternally free

Standing at the gates of heaven invited
Trembling knowing I will be delighted

Knowing I cannot enter without permission
In life the requirement is submission

Breaching the gates of heaven tonight
Waiting aside there to share delight

So joyful its hard to stand
Entering slowly is the plan

Rejoicing that we are connected
No fear to be denied or rejected

This is the place of my dream
Sure it would be all it seem

Hoping to enter not needing a pass
Here to fulfill my desires at last

Although closed upon arrival
Know that inside was eternal survival

Upon entry receiving constant joy
Here there would be nothing better than mo'

Where all my life I longed to be
At last released and knowing me

Fresh dew upon the grass
Grateful journey finished at last

It is here one taste the fruit of the tree
This is where one lives eternally free

RIVERS OF GOLD

From rivers of gold flows life's essence
Whenever it happens it's a blessing

For you alone I will give the gold
Once was young but now old

When it comes to the gate
Hoping that I am not too late

No matter what the path it follows
It is like the mine, the shaft shallow

Always willing to share
As a way of living to care

Blessed is the thoughts each day
Leading to happiness showing the way

As we dream the night away
Hoping to share morning the day

Understanding that there is one
Willing to wait for another sun

Here comes the morning dew
Which results from joining two

When one wishing the golden river ride
Appreciating the wonders one side by side

Like the blowing wind yearning
Puts out the hottest fire burning

When it reaches the end
Thoughts of it again and again

From rivers of gold flows life's essence
Whenever it happens it's a blessing

LAND OF GOLD

I speak to you of a land of gold
The complete story has yet to be told

It is the place we find one of mother's great empires
Out of it came Mali and Songhai but it was their sire

In the near time it was by England oppressed
Until the people rose to this harm redressed

The freedom savior was by them led
Within him a pan African ideology bred

He was Saturday born first child of his mother
Destined to lead, follow uplift each other

There is a place, a city Accra called
Here find the traditional now the house walled

Their memory of the coup forgotten by the freedom park
Returning the visitor and the forgotten now happily walk

It some point the invaders named it the coast
This came about as it provided the rings about which we boast

There is a river where those in chains bathed
Walking in the water many died the only way to be saved

Here the visitors now feet bare stalked
To honor the many thousand gone do not talk

Along the edge of the ocean where concentration camps existed
They are called Elmina, Christiansborg, and others where died who resisted

Here is a space for the captives to be held
There they are beaten, raped, branded, and jailed

When the ships arrived they are boarded
Through the gate of no return to be loaded

Stacked and racked no room no space
Slavers objective to cram and ram in place

Now to ride over the ocean tormented abused
The humanity of the captives continually refused

Resisting throughout the process thousands will not survive
Some jump into the ocean revolt doing what freedom required

Upon arrival treated as stock in a strange land
There beaten, shackled, paraded and branded

On this day many thousands have returned
Those whose ancestors taken to a place to be spurned

This is the story of the world's first and only race
Taken from the place of creation the life's base

Brought to a land of the free and brave
Made into a place progress was based on the enslave

While at home the colonized fought to over come
Then one day in 1957 the battle Osagyefo won

I speak to you of a land of gold
The complete story has yet to be told

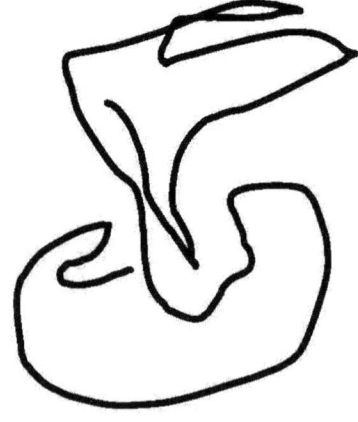

OUR GOLD MINE

We travel golden streets each to mine
Through the heavenly gates to find

When two have a goal
It finds its relief in gold

Then the pain has soul
Apart it takes a toll

Outside the gates cold
Requesting entry must be bold

The way is tender like a roll
It is best entered holding a pole

The desire is to write on the scroll
When open and not when fold

The gold in my hand I hold
Although hard it is soft to mold

Out of the mine children never to be sold
Thought many hoped to deny and be untold

When accessing the mine diamonds not coal
Joined in the shaft nothing stole

AFRICAN MINE

There is a place on the coast of cape
Where here hue people were locked and raped

A castle fort built strong
The owners protected as they did wrong

A door leading to the sea
A ship waiting to pack knee to knee

From the land of gold
Hue mans were taken to the hold

There were oppressors' rooms at the mine
Where the captured were not allowed to dine

A fortification built on the coast
Where many in the sun did roast

On the top of the mound
There the fort is found

Weeping and gnashing of teeth
Men women and child shackled feet

A special place for those who rebelled
Not fed, nor clothed until death in the cell

THE WEEPING TREE

The tree of life weeps
Weeps for those who are it peeps
Peeps whose life force it keeps
Keeps from them one who feed reaps
Reaps the good into whose soil seeps
Seeps when exposed to creeps
Creeps from place to place then leaps
Leaps over the grass and the heaps
Heaps of leaves and mounds deep

The cut when healed hides
Hides the scar upon it continually resides
Resides with cuts, cut sides
Sides torn with tears rolling like tides
Tides of pain like life in the tree abides

There the weeping tree sits
Sits for all to see hoping
Hoping for a time to be not
Not to harm it is the key for both
Both occurs windward and lee crying
Crying occurs whether cut or broken purposely
Purposely understanding that tears sooth tree and thee
Thee cut it branches and it weeps like we
We shed these are tears for those not free

The branch when cut crying
Crying tears run until they dry
Dry the branches and leaves dying
Dying leaves fall the bird flying
Flying away as the tree sighs

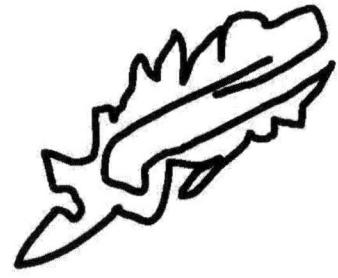

NEEDING MO

Every day needing mo
Without so there is a feeling low
Even when there is enough, so
A feeling of desperation and woe
Like a car that fails needing a tow
Overcame no energy just slow
It happened why don't know

With mo feeling the wind blow
As it moves over, a glow
Although the answer is yes, no
Unable to move trying to go
Without like plowing without a hoe
The dew on the grass ready to mow
Each day needing mo

IF YOU LEFT

No longer together tears I cry
Seems that lonely desire is to die

If you left for another me
The future I will not see

When alone without you
Don't know what I'd do

You made my life complete
Without you no victories only defeat

Together we found the way
Lost and alone bereft, night, no day

On the day when you gone
Desire for weus still strong

Tried to pretend you still here
Sensing panic all is fear

For every change there is a cause
Not knowing what happened pause

No longer together tears I cry
Seems that lonely desire is to die

TO KISS YOUR LIPS

A taste of heaven so sweet
Pleasure and magic replete

When our lips meet
Slow breathing rapid heartbeat

Although at times wet or dry
Always the taste fulfills my desire

Whether covered or plain
Continues to my desire sustain

Lips to lips a forever dream
Coming together smooth like cream

They are to me like magic
Not connecting them tragic

My lips your lips seek
Temperature rising reaching a peak

As they meet what a taste
Slowly moving without haste

A fulfilled promise perfect match
Together found like lock and catch

Coming together at last
Moving in rhythm not fast

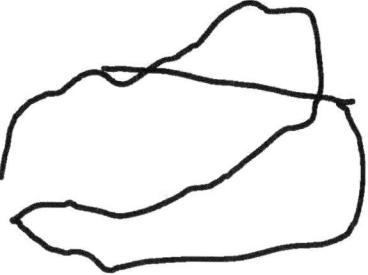

An air that is full of happy sounds
In my heart drumming resounds

One without the other apart
In synch like beat and heart

Coming together pure bliss
Causing the juices to flow during the tryst

A taste of heaven so sweet
Pleasure and magic replete

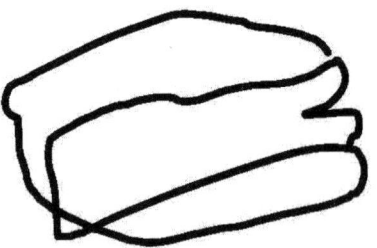

WIND AND SPIRIT

The wind and the spirit in unity ignites
Together unified joined weus excites

There is a wind that blows
A spirit intuitively that knows

Wind in the clear cooling air
Spirit unknown for us to share

The wind rages over the head as if a gale
Internal the spirit for us comes without fail

Upon the winds of life happiness is joy
Spirits acknowledges that there is more

There are mo words upon the wind today
Speaking of the sweetness showing the way

The wind whispers of a magic spell
The spirits tell of coming o so well

The wind is the father, the sire
The spirit is the mother, the burning fire

The wind and the spirit in unity ignites
Together joined unified weus excites

COLLMINE

Her name is Collmine
She is an African queen
Her like has never been seen

Woman of gold
Has a healing soul
A story yet untold

Of her you proud would be
She is something to see
Wonderful daughter of He

Strives every day to make the world better
Now a woman of poetry and letters
A real artist, creative and willing go-getter

Collmine Is a lady of delight
Reaching for higher and higher heights
Has a spirit that brings the light

Today I present her to you
She is our perfection that is true
On a path prepared for just a few

She is a golden child
A lady of such style
A daughter of the Nile
Her name is Collmine
She is an African queen
Her like has never been seen

I FEEL THE

I feel the fire of your presence
When you come I become alive

I feel the heat of our union
Then we join in the heat of us

It is the time of emotional explosion
We connect like match to striker

The flame of our emotions
Connecting to bring extreme pleasure

A touch ignites the spark to flame
Burning so hot that it consumes

In your presence a consuming sensation
Sensing that heat becomes hottest with you

Together our union combustion
When we touch a flame ignited

This burning began at first sight
Flames lasting until time endless

The last embrace of the night
A dream where gates were lifted

MORE

My greatest pleasure is to please as we plead for more
Feelings joining as the morning mist
Fades to become the new day
Taking the pleasure of pleasing
To unknown heights
Assisting the barriers to break as two merge
The rivers of our thought flow
Unaltered into one truth
Wanting becomes having becomes had
Knowing becomes known as the journey
Reaches its climax
Our great pleasure was to please as we pled for more
Totally enveloped within your tender titillating touch
Experiencing the expression of your excellence
Search our souls for the substance
Of its substantiation
Dedicate our desire to determine the depth of its diligence
Delight in our drive as we determine the direction and distance
Delving into the depth of your deliciousness more

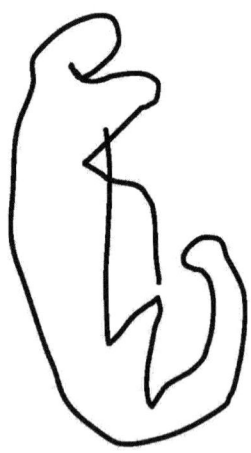

ON THE PATH

Today on the path I saw you walking
In my dream with you I was talking

Longing for your physical presence
In my spirit I communed with your essence

As you passed me by sudden breeze
In a moment a smile weakened knees

Yesterday on the path together we came
In my dream with you joined in the rain

Longing for your hand in mine
In my spirit we merged like a rhyme

As you passed the whiff of your perfume
In a moment all my senses consumed

Tomorrow on the path blessed we will meet
In our dream moments of happiness as we greet

Longing for your essence in our bliss
In our spirit touching holding we kiss

As you passed through my life joy without measure
In a moment time after time your presence pleasure

CARING SOUNDS OF

Each morning I wake with anticipation longing to hear your voice
I wake from the soundless fast of a night without your present
Then I break the fast to you as my sustenance
The caring sound of you sustains my spirit
My spirit is energized by the magic of your sound
Your voice ends my lonely nights
This sound is gentle and invigorates my physical self
As the morning wanes I began to anticipate the evening
For here I prepare for another infusion of you
The evening is a caring place culmination in soothing sounds
Here comes the night of fasting to await the morning caring sounds of…

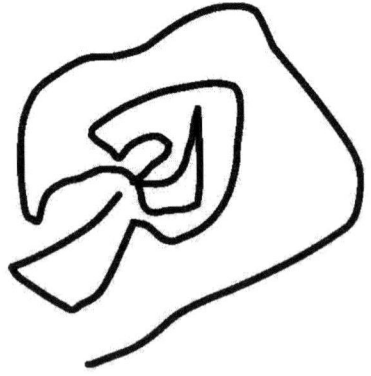

LOVE TO

Love to walk in the woods would that you will be there as we talk
Love to dance the two-step stepping to the beat of our hearts
Love to read the words of love loving to connect with the disconnected
Love to prepare dishes to titillate delicious the taste
Love to join jointly with knowing knowledge
Love to make my breath breathless as the lungs long air
Love to be the spirit spiriting us on the path to finding
Love to come together coming together in union
Love to sing songs of significance as we see our sound
Love to reveal revelation deep within the depth
Love to find miracles miraculous alteration which changes everything
Love to the destination destiny to complete the journey
Love to love in loving is the way to perfection

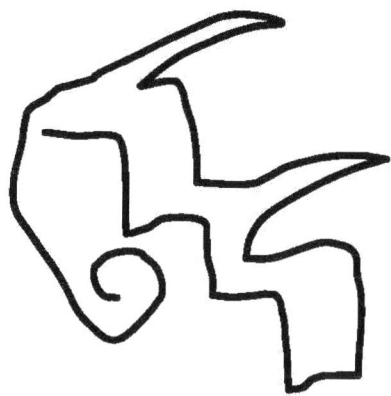

WHY

Why when I saw you I saw us
This is when my memory was revived

The many encounters remain alive
Within this meeting our spirits greet

Today is the culmination of our beginning
Yesterday was a collection of our ends

Our emotions are the reflection of encounter
What we know is the fusion of what we knew

Across the wide divide of time space
Long fingers of memory are again reawakened

I know you and you know I know
Why when I said you I remember seeing

OKRA'S SPOON

I long to be scooped by your spoon
When, never too soon
Whether it be table or a tea
Just as long as it is me
Take me in your hand
Hold me tight like a rubber band
Take a little taste
Never in haste
Sip me with lovely lips
Hold me tight to your hips
This is all I desire
Lovely one quench my fire
Your spoon I would fill neatly
Ready to be consumed completely
I long to be scooped by your spoon

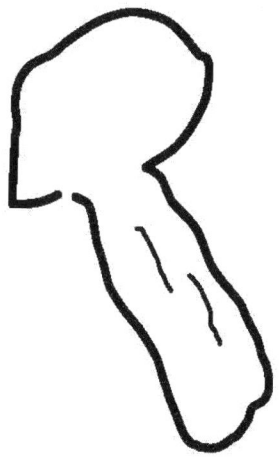

NOW IS OUR TIME

Now is the time to put one thought after the other
Our time to think the thoughts of you and me, of us
As we connect now is our time
Coming alive it is our joy we find
Now is the time to put one thought after the other
Our time to think the thoughts of you and me, of us
We have been apart too long
The moments of us coming, a simple song
Now is the time to put one thought after the other
Our time to think the thoughts of you and me, of us
Wishing in my alone I am able you to touch
When holding your hand, feeling your face is not too much
Now is the time to put one thought after the other
Our time to think the thoughts of you and me, of us
In this space where only us
There find the connection we trust
Now is the time to put one thought after the other
Our time to think the thoughts of you and me, of us
Together we are joined at last
Here are all the ALL that completes our task
Now is the time to put one thought after the other
Our time to think the thoughts of you and me, of us
No questions need to be asked today
All that we do together follows the way
Now is the time to put one thought after the other
Our time to think the thoughts of you and me, of us

I and you became the us without doubt
That joined to the world we can shout
Now is the time to put one thought after the other

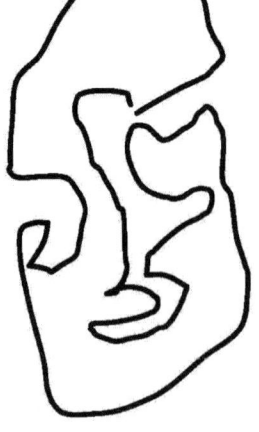

Our time to think the thoughts of you and me, of us
Missing your beauty in this place
Time now to come and fill the space
Now is the time to put one thought after the other
Our time to think the thoughts of you and me, of us

KEMET LOVERS

In Kemet land two souls were revealed
Walking separate paths two to one sealed
Each time thinking of Kemet across the sea
This is where my baby's love met thee
It is an ancient land goddess there met you
Holy is the place where came one out of two
In the hallowed halls two alone walked
When traversed these spaces lovers talked
Together lovers walked land in hand
Where met united in the holy land
Ancestors called lovers come near
Decision to understand that joining clear
Both early decided desire to quell
Spirits destressed needing to be well
Once lovers knew what love knew
Together on hallowed sands renewed
Love came upon them as sounds like thunder
Joined two to one never to be asunder
They joined two not a blunder
It is that which is to be without rejection

I THINK OF MY BABY

When I think of you my heart sings
I hear the notes of love they ring
Lonely are the moments when apart
Aching is the feeling within my heart
The way to join lovers heart is clear
Each step taken brings us near
Many waste what is love not knowing life
Many days in emotional strife
There is no pleasure in the world alone
Only a sense senseless heavy like stone
Each day thinking of the ancestors more
For the pleasure in love so much joy
My love lovingly together we write
Attempting to bring words of love in sight
Like the sands of sandy space thine
Number so numerous loving thoughts mine
Only the lonely moments come to an end
When time timeless the union can mend

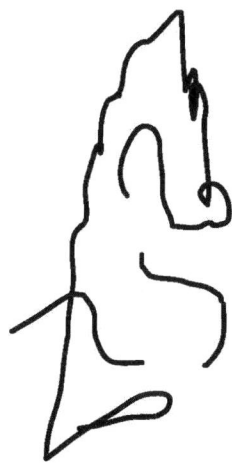

ARMS OF LOVE

In the arms of my love I cease to be
Be separate and alone as I become one
One who in the mist of us finds bliss
Bliss as a space where a mystery of life is
Is where is solved the unknown joy
Joy of joining two into one connected
Connected combined creation of perfect loving
Loving perfectly reduces the better to best
Best is the shared vision when we are united
United in winding entwined moments arms within arms
Arms of my love where disconnection cease to be

DREAMS OF US

Today I woke dreaming of you
Being by your side is one out of two
One day away from us makes me blue
Each moment is too many not a few
My desire for you does not lessen it grew
I know that each feeling is not old but new
In my daydreams I see my baby one of hue
Ancestors gave me my desire fidelity is my due
Early I did not know why I loved not a clue
My life revealed not unanswered under review
Now I am committed to love within this milieu
Today I am awake dreaming of you

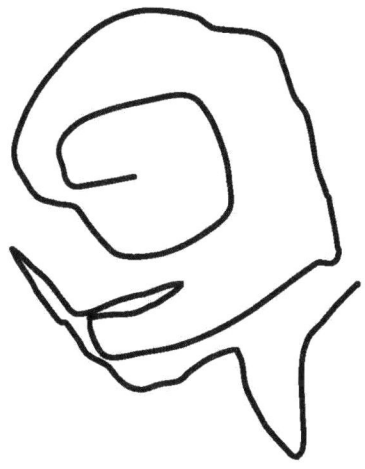

SHIP ON THE OCEAN

Love is like a ship on the ocean
Like a boat on the sea
The only true love is between you and me

Deep is the touch when sharing truth
Wet are the tears streaking the face

Each stroke pulls the waves of wetness
Deeply the blowing tides push to the limit

It tosses and turns as it cuts through the waves
Waves that pitch and yawl together rising

Reaching the highest heights it slides
Through each wave reaching its peak

Love then is wet rolling through the storm
Perfect love comes in the eye awaiting the whirlwind

Love is like a ship on the ocean
Like a boat on the sea
The only true love is between you and me

CAN'T WAIT

Can hardly wait to see you again
It is hard constantly thinking of when

My feelings flow like the waters wild
South to north confluence with your smile

As I prepare for our soon to be
Rushing like the wind joining you I see

Thoughts of two into one coming
United in our spirit additions oneing

In my heart feeling of great sadness
A gift of healing to give you some gladness

Regret the time it took to get you
Missing the years of your blessing too

Between each moment our blessings reside
All that we need is where us choose to abide

Leaving you again no matter we reject
When finally again us connect

WITHOUT STRUGGLE

O what a day to be in your life
An end to confusion received without strafe

Each morning comes with the dew
Upon the grass refreshing love anew

Awake my love and I come together
United tightly in each other's arms like feathers

Refreshing is the warmth surrounding the two
Merging together is the intermingle like new

As time passes the intensity grow
No question perfect loving both know

We welcome the evening time
Joining in bliss delight we find

Now its nighttime for our dreams
This is where the couple discover what love means

O what will a new day be in our life
Time to express love together without strife

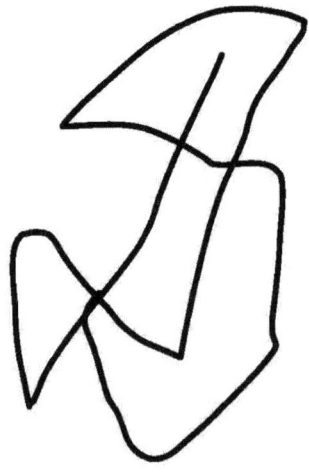

THE LETTER

Today I felt you sent me a letter
Writing words that made me feel better

Though each day to you I speak
Sending the written words especially unique

As I opened the letter that I need
The special way you write my desires feed

The envelope's message began with its stamp
Igniting my anticipation like light to lamp

The content matched the many words clear
Words only we would share without fear

Baby began and ended the salutation
Endearing words that connected our relation

The many-colored paper was chosen blank
Words to connect building each plank

Words of love words of life
Upon each page they slice like a knife

The beginning as all life in the dark
The ending complete with a mark

TONIGHT

This is the last of our first nights
Next occasion is already in sight

We part with anticipation of being lonely
Though we continue to yearn for each solely

Tomorrow we leave to take flight
To the air separated by only sight

Soon we shall journey to our space
Making a way to find this loving place

O how I miss you my true charm
Only place I yearn to be is arm in arm

Tonight I will read our love book
Containing only that which we found in a look

Today is a waste without you
It is one moment devoid of two

Just the thought of you made my dream
Always longing for your presence it seem

Come to me my only love true
I need to be with you as sky is to blue

LOVERS WELL MET

Each time thinking of Kemet across the sea
This is where loving well met thee

It is a goddess land perfect there met you
Holy is the place where came one out of two

In the hallowed halls alone walked
When traversed these spaces lovers talked

Together lovers walked hand in hand
Where well met united in the holy land

Ancestors called lovers to come near
They understand that joining is clear

Both early decided desire to quell
Two spirits needing to be well

Once lovers knew what love knew
Walked together on the sacred sands renewed

Love came upon them as lighting and thunder
Joined two to one never to be asunder

This joining resulting in spirit connection
That which is to be without rejection

HEART SINGS

When I think of you my heart sings
I hear the notes of love they ring

Lonely are the moments when apart
Aching is the feeling within my heart

The way to join lovers' heart is clear
Each step taken brings us near

There is no pleasure in the world alone
Only a sense senseless heavy like stone

Each day thinking of the ancestors more
For the presence of us in love much joy

Many waste what is love not knowing life
Unknowingly conflicting words cause strife

My love lovingly together we write
Attempting to bring words of love in sight

Only the lonely moments come to an end
When time is timeless the union can mend

MY BABY (MINE)

I bring to you songs of a singer my baby mine
Her voice is sugar sweet so very fine

Sounds that thrill thrilling my soul
When I hear the melodious melody hot not cold

I bring to you songs of a singer mine
Her voice is sugar sweet so very fine

Through the windless wind my baby blows
Into the lighting lights notes glows

I bring to you songs of a singer mine
Her voice is sugar sweet so very fine

When my baby sings songs of love and affection
Our spirits join jointly in love's reflection

I bring to you songs of a singer mine
Her voice is sugar sweet so very fine

To the world in worldly language my baby scream
Expressing love expressly perfectly it seems

I bring to you songs of a singer mine
Her voice is sugar sweet so very fine

Reverberating reverberations that alter alterations
Founded foundations which inspire inspiration

I bring to you songs of a singer mine
Her voice is sugar sweet so very fin

The songs my baby sing are freshly refreshing unbound
Vocals vocalizing and reconnecting perfect sound

I bring to you songs of a singer my baby mine
Her voice is sugar sweet so very fine

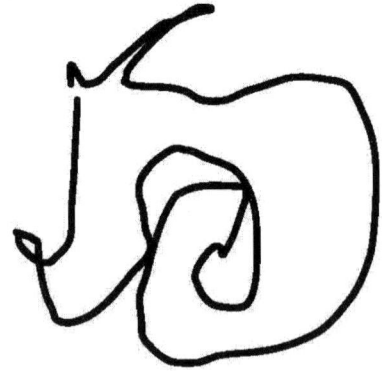

INFINITY

Our love will an infinity last
From now until the future is the past

Two eights occurring twice
Infinity is doubled nice

From now until then
Here to when

All that was and will be
More than all eyes can see

From the root to top of the tree
Shore to across the wide sea

From brief inhale
To the blowing gale

Our love will an infinity last
From now until the future is the past

EXCUSE

I look to your protest
There I found a reason for redress
In your actions an excuse
There a foundation and reason to recuse
Every way you show my error
Using laws and even terror
Within the movement an excuse found
Another way to escape or get around
Looking for a way to continue my life
Working to suppress some without strife
Although it is a new day
For some it just the same old way
Those who use history as an excuse for oppression
Are those who tend to plan for regression
The flag as an excuse to ignore hate
Come to equity oh so late
The use of strength to suppress
This is the excuse to address
Those who use the bully pulpit preserve
As an excuse to bully the underserved

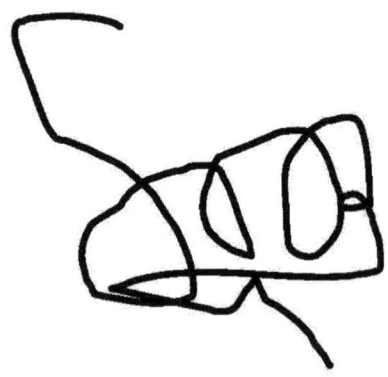

MAYBE

Maybe we are more may than be
Maybe you no longer love me
Maybe you no longer truly see
Maybe you care no longer
Maybe you are weak not strong
Maybe you can't see the us in we
Maybe you can't see the want for need
Maybe our caring is fading away
Maybe our togetherness is only this day
Maybe what we want is not in us
Maybe what we want is trust
Maybe what we need is from another
Maybe what we need is a mother
Maybe we are more may than be

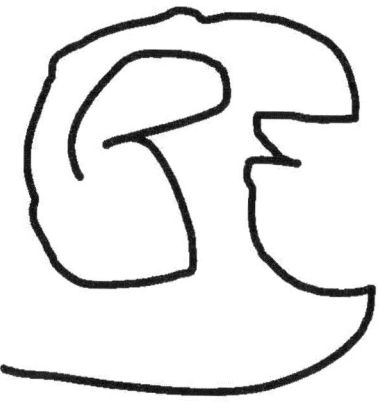

INTO THE DEEP

The killers dropped the bodies down
In the deep blue, white capped
Bloody are the hands that row
Although the sails shine
Bleached white by equators sun
They march from east to west
Under the lash streaming blood
Chained and bound degraded
Men women and children all
Lined upon the red stained sand

They came with the promise
Of wealth untold and a new world
Said what they thought was good to hear
In their heart a satanic endeavor
Taking the best of the best
Cared not if adult or infant
Treated them not as human but things
Was bargained in exchange for items
Willing to engage as long as not their own
Through the door last time on the land

Down through many fathoms to ground
Below the waves until life sapped
These are those without wind that make it go
See so reflective they blind
In contrast to the whipped blood that runs
Taken are the communities best
Somewhere in the future the hood
Heads bashed and cracked never braided

Killed left to rot those that fall
Some who resisted losing a hand

A regal people designated
Took the best and left the rest
An effort twofold in endeavor
Taking one group to lessen the other
Thus the conquest of both
With the blow of whip and deceit
Making the way for future exploitation
Of the land and people too
Came those from a dying place
To kill the source of life and liberty

VEGAN COFFEE

Coffee is best served from an ebony pot
Brewed over a fire 'til hot

Like an explosion flavor burst forth
Making the effort is of worth

It is enhanced with nondairy cream
Smooth and mellow its favor seem

The beans can be ground by hand
Taking extra effort is the plan

Brewing excites the sense of smell
Closer it gets to ready it swells

When ready placed upon the table
Ready to be sipped swallows when able

All come together perfectly content
Like a racer at the end spent

Consuming as watching the dawn
Sitting outside dew on the lawn

Coffee is best served from an ebony pot
Brewed over a fire 'til hot

AFTERNOON TEA

Now is the time for afternoon tea
Joining satisfying both you and me
Sharing what quenches our thirst with glee

Today is the time for a treat
Even those who wish to eat
Assume that the evening is desire replete

It comes together bright like sun burst
When the need is to quench the thirst
Running to the table get there first

Together with the sweet cake
Eating all of what we bake
Fulfilling all desire for joy's sake

Time to join we us well met
Sharing the afternoon dividing what's wet
We are always performing on the set

This is what we do in the afternoon
Meeting and splitting joy not too soon
Every day to have the tea is a boom

KILLING ROSES

Three bullets fly
On the street a rose dies

Today blessed with the blue
Tonight I hunt the hue

Shoot to kill
What a thrill

The flower of youth pass
Now complete is my task

Crowd chant I'm wrong
But that's just a song

What happened in the night
Members of the club always right

Wait until protester tire
Time will put out their ire

Although this job I may lose
Ending the story here is what I choose

STORY OF THE REED

This is the story of the reed
Bowing before the high wind
Not selfish caring for his need
Bending his knee again and again

When others stand
Would you continue to kneel
If they refuse to shake your hand
Can you continue to express how you feel

This is the story of the reed
Bowing before the high wind
Not selfish caring for his need
Bending his knee again and again

When they you refuse to hire
Although you have skills they need
Will it influence your desire
Are you worried about those you feed

This is the story of the reed
Bowing before the high wind
Not selfish caring for his need
Bending his knee again and again

Is this the story of the brave
Or can you confront those who oppress
Refusing to give up acting as a slave
Continuing to demand total redress

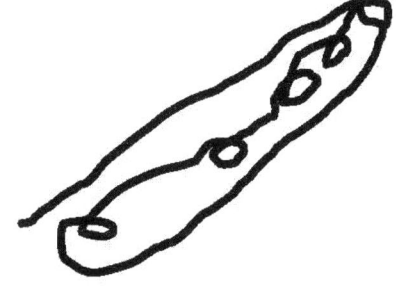

This is the story of the reed
Bowing before the high wind
Not selfish caring for his need
Bending his knee again and again

If someday the story is told
His name beside Cap will be displayed
How whatever the cost refused to fold
Stood and delivered did not cave

This is the story of the reed
Bowing before the high wind
Not selfish caring for his need
Bending his knee again and again

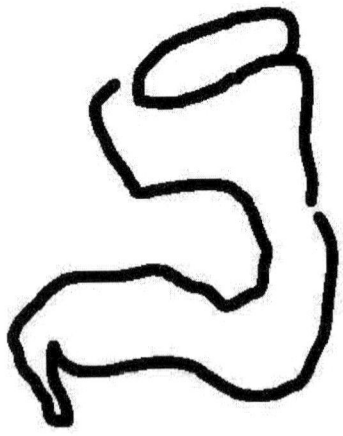

SALUTING THE SUN

Reaching for the sky
Stretching don't know why

Hands together as in prayer
Fingertips touching there

Then we roll them toward the face
Close they came reverse the space

Body bending low at the waist
Hand touching the ground for a taste

Take one foot move it to the rear
Another is moved both rest there

Then both of the knees touch
On the ground not too much

The body is aligned like a plank
Hold the pose like soldiers in rank

Sliding forward moving in line much like a snake
Face and chest bending upward and cobra make

The head is downward facing
The midsection upward bracing

One foot snapping moves forward
The other matches it is coming toward

This is the way to in half bend
Head touching knees almost the end

Come full to align like an arrow
Straight the body is glad no sorrow

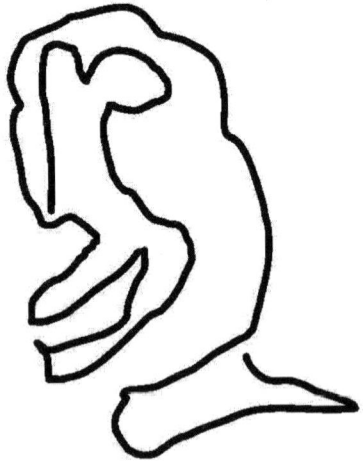

THE BOWL SINGS TO THEE

Your spirit is found in your singing bowl
Playing it reflects those who hold

It helps to communicate on a spiritual plane
Hears the internal voice clear making energy plain

Tells the many stories of my spirit
Explains clearly for one seeking near it

As the mallet goes around
Makes a wondrous sound

Created by masters in prayer
Constructed in their rarified air

This is the essence of the flow
Works better when prayers grow

Pulls from the essence of soul
Revealing an etheric story yet untold

The more the bowl chime
It does with sound my life find

It tells the story you do not know
Singing it your many chakras show

As it is played in the advent of night
It sounds out of darkness the light

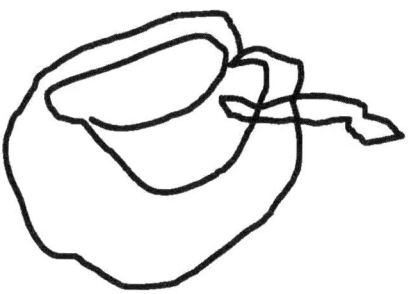

A sound that reduces the impact of stress
Portends to the hearer a chance for rest

Some players receive well being
As it stimulates and improves seeing

Allows us the sounds to feel
Now we know life vibrations are real

Clears the mind and strengthens peace
Gives a sense of clarity and anxiety release

Many players acknowledge helps with pain
This occurs as sounds speak to the brain

Engages mindful meditation
Reflects the practitioner's dedication

It helps to communicate on a spiritual plane
Hears the voice clear making energy plain

This is your singing bowl
Playing it reflects those who hold

HOUSE OF TIME

In the distance high against the sky
Built by ancestors to answer why

There they stand for all humanity
To reify that Africans will forever be

Block upon block laid by hand
Massive yet simple 'til today they stand

Believed to be the house of the body at rest
Ravaged and relieved of its riches until reader's request

The expectation was not would come the savage
Breaking and entering many possessions to ravage

Contents taken spread far and wide
That which saved for after the after laid with pride

What was needed to make the journey complete
Taken by robbers bragging full with conceit

One day the children will with memory returned
Reading letters which were with holy writers interned

Mer by some called house of fire
Constructed to protect eternal desire

Salvation resurrection is for all
Whether king queen noble servant called

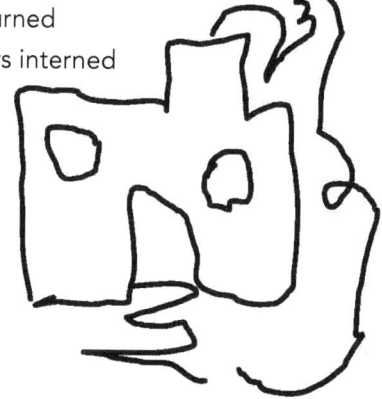

Those who built sent a message clear
That eternal life is nothing to fear

We are and ever will be people of the way
Confused and enslaved minds until today

Never again to be led into the night
With the SaRa as the guiding light

PERIOD OF TIME

There was a period of time
When you became mine
On the road to lonely a sign
Took me back to be thine
Many a day you could hear me opine
That is until the path to you I could find
Here is where I focus on you on my mind
No distractions morning or night always divine
Without you unknowingly daily for you I pine
As written love words each and every line
To me they draw you closer our spirits bind
Making nothing into something is a grind
Always you to me like a frog's hair you are fine
Now you and me mo of the same kind
This was the period of time

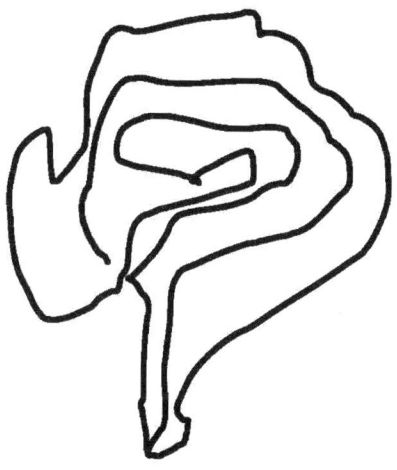

TRANSITION

Now is the time
Used all of the earthly mine

Walked the path true
Doing what I was supposed to do

Listen my life was great
Used most with a perfect mate

Able to have children two
Who then grands gave a few

The way leads to the end
Now is time for life to begin

The journey is to the light
A path that is full and bright

Future explained by those in the past
That which is desired will forever last

Weep if necessary only a little while
Spend the time thinking of our life with a smile

WATERWAY

Traveling along the nile
To my heart filled I smile
It is the highway that the mers bring
Along which the mourners and worshipers sing

There the nile that is blue
Rolling water coming in true

Traveling along the nile
To my heart filled I smile
It is the highway that the mers bring
Along which the mourners and worshipers sing

There is a nile that is white
Rolling waters on what is right

Traveling along the nile
To my heart filled I smile
It is the highway that the mers bring
Along which the mourners and worshipers sing

One begins at a place a lake
Slowly growing a trickle a stream it make

Traveling along the nile
To my heart filled I smile
It is the highway that the mers bring
Along which the mourners and worshipers sing

Another from a mountain moon

Slowly collecting to a river soon

Traveling along the nile
To my heart filled I smile
It is the highway that the mers bring
Along which the mourners and worshipers sing

It rolls for many thousand miles
Ever traveling resources giving all the while

Traveling along the nile
To my heart filled I smile
It is the highway that the mers bring
Along which the mourners and worshipers sing

She travels both the dead and living
All the while essential assistance giving

Traveling along the nile
To my heart filled I smile
It is the highway that the mers bring
Along which the mourners and worshipers sing

The waters are the great divide
Leaving rich the soil when subside

Traveling along the nile
To my heart filled I smile
It is the highway that the mers bring
Along which the mourners and worshipers sing

Those whose spirit would wealthy be
When possible should journey to nile see

Traveling along the nile
To my heart filled I smile
It is the highway that the mers bring
Along which the mourners and worshipers sing

A road that fed the intellect of many thousands gone
Developed religion, education, philosophy lasting and strong

BURNT PEOPLE LAND

High in the hills
Its height gives me thrills
In the valley deep
Walking there you I seek
The hot air is oh so dry
Longing for it to pass me by
Sun shines on my face
Rising is the temperature in this place
Beads roll down from the heat
Too much feeling like I'm beat
This is a day in the burnt people land
Here we are fulfilled where we stand
What a joy to walk on holy ground
To seek the beginning of life found

People they smile
Dressed in wondrous style
Venders on the street
Wares stacked and neat
What a wondrous sight
Smells of lunch a delight
When the music play
Oh how they dance all day
Touching when lights are low
On how they romance moving slow
Dinkinesh just give me a chance
It is you I wish to romance

BUTTERFLY

If I could fly like the butterfly
Where would I go
What would I do
Who would I be
When would I fly

I feel the flapping wings
That cool the ardor of my yearning
See the color of blue
Expressing the sadness of separation
Taste the bitterness of time
Unsweet is the flavor without you hearing the sound cry

If I could fly like the butterfly
Where would I go
What would I do
Who would I be
When would I fly

These feelings are without compare
Never seen the image of you fly
Lying there upon the air silent
Screaming that I am here for you
There we are joined in our reality
Of emptiness in the space that you occupy

If I could fly like the butterfly
Where would I go
What would I do
Who would I be

When would I fly

A moving motion in motion moving
It flies behind me flying to the lead
There it is but I don't see it there blind
The painter's colors on colors of my canvas
Brilliant out standing out nothing it lacks all

WEEDING AND SEEDING

Living and transition both are needed
Just as the garden is watered and seeded

The need to survive is universal
Losing the time is reversal

Those who typically choose to survive
Are born with all they need to thrive

It begins with the first breath
Ends if of air we are bereft

Need that which to each energy provide
Used to regenerate the essence inside

Although different for many their remnants
A covering to protect from the elements

There are some who reside under stars
Others need to build many walls with bars

Engaging in acts to continue generations
Coming together with rules unique for situations

Those who act to fulfill this need
Are those who in actions take the lead

Few exist for long who ignore the drive
They take the journey into energy alive

Many wish loved one could stay
Would have them here forever and a day

Although some feel an end with the khat
Believers understand this is not that

Know when the body sheds the ka
It also through separation moves the ba

There are many who choose to eat what's dead
Upon the refuse decaying they are fed

Living and transition both are needed
Just as the garden is watered and seeded

CUTTING BRANCHES

There is a tree that weeps
It is one that when it grows it leaps
It begins when planted a twig
After a few years it is big

Proper water, soil, and sun
What you get is growth just begun
Special leaves on its branches grow
When blows the future it sows

The cycle itself repeats
From seed to twig to tree complete
Fully developed its branches swing
In the storm hard blowing bring

In the cycle of life a giant made
Telling all that each seed is laid
The trunk its skin shed
Branches broken in time bled

Over the moments they heal
As the sap leaking congeal
Look to the tree as metaphor of life
Through patience and care heal strife

STEP ON EVIL

There is a way to stand
A way one places the hand

Since the time before time
Our bodies sent the message alive
Here we find nesi amsu
Removing evil it's a stance true

When the statue is made
A memorial to those who never fade
Here we find nesi amsu
Removing evil it's a stance true

Whether in the building we hide
Or set upon the outer side
Here we find nesi amsu
Removing evil it's a stance true

Let those who in this world long
Remind us and them of those gone
Here we find nesi amsu
Removing evil it's a stance true

As the figure is left at the place
It informs that there remains a space
Here we find nesi amsu
Removing evil it's a stance true

When we choose the way of right
It reinfuses overcoming the dark with light

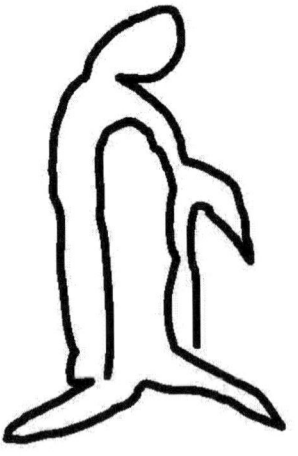

Here we find nesi amsu
Removing evil it's a stance true

It matters not the coming of wrong
No one can ignore the voices and song
Here we find nesi amsu
Removing evil it's a stance true

In the end we all will smile
Waiting for the joy all the while

I DON'T KNOW

I awake without the memory of Who I am
Who I am, I know what I am called
I know the limited history communicated
To me by my caretakers
I know what they related
Concerning this place
What is remembered by them
Is their truth which becomes my truth

I do not know from whence I come
What I did or did not do
I have no idea of why I exist now
I don't know

What I do know is that my mission
Is to understand at the very least
Who I am

What I am is apart from
What I do
What I say and what I believe
Is apart from me
Although each of these are component
Of the one, me I do not know
They are not me

Each day I don't receive information of me
Each night in what I have been told are dreams
I receive bits and pieces of another life
I am not sure that this other life is me or

I am this other life

Is the truth connecting the two
Am I separated apart from what happens
In the sleep state
Where do we go when we
Go where we are going

We cannot know until we get there
When we get there will we know that
We are there or will we
Look forward to going
Where we are going
It is possible that the going is all there is
If in fact the going is the getting there
Then we must keep going
Do the doing during the going in order to
Accomplish anything on the journey

If we miss the opportunity
To do during the doing
Then we waste the opportunity to be
Thus it is the doing during the going
That allows us to be
This is the true essence of living
Loving and longing
This is the manifestation of Creator and
Weus together
It is always the doing
The doing in order to get
To the going to do again

You can face temptation and
Resist because the picture you

Have to more significant to you
What you see in the physical world
Is temporal what you feel
Spiritual and cannot be
Disappointed by the mere
Thought process
It is deep within the needs

All may desire physical but it is temporary and
Unsatisfying to truly be
Satisfied you must have in loving
Loving for the one you love
Provides a reassurance that
What you have is necessary
What you don't is unnecessary
I don't know

VOICES I HEAR

The sound of one call 'til hoarse
A mother to child of course

The screams of a parent at the game
Win or lose enthused just the same

Whispers of a lover at dawn
Hold your heart in the voice like a pawn

There are sweet nothings as we walk on the beach
Bodies swaying with the breeze just within reach

Exacerbated is the sound when yes or no
Articulating the reason to stay or go

Excited in the moments not of a few
Like the early morning grass wet with dew

In the many moments of our dreams
So involved it overwhelms the scene

Whether it comes soft or hard voice
When I hear it speak makes me her choice

RESARECTION

The son was not erect
Upright and able to protect

Some say it was not a bright sun
Other believed that it was the one

Many say built of wood
There you found it firm stood

We find the ones made of stone
Many placed in temples to atone

Now we find them on graves
Those who need them a path paved

Written on the stone words of grace
To prove what was built not from space

Some reveal the fruit's seed
That the spirit infused the deed

The pinnacle now has been told
Ben two placed upon it a cap of gold

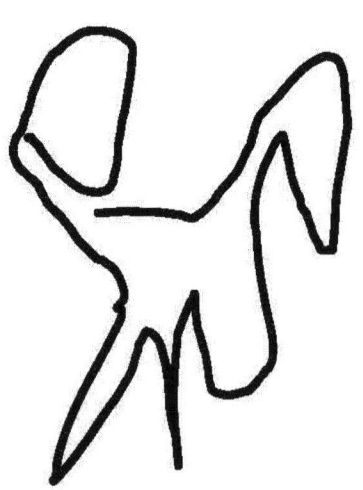

HERD

This is the movement of the herd
Mimicking in silence speaking not a word

When the leader raises the head
All follow and move unless dead

They follow the movement in unity
Together working like its duty

In lockstep whether in love or fear
All seem to move in direction clear

From days of birth until grown
This instinct of union is hone

There is no individual response call
The group is superior over all

Doing what the leaders direct
Followers mirror them being correct

This is the movement of the herd
Mimicking in silence speaking not a word

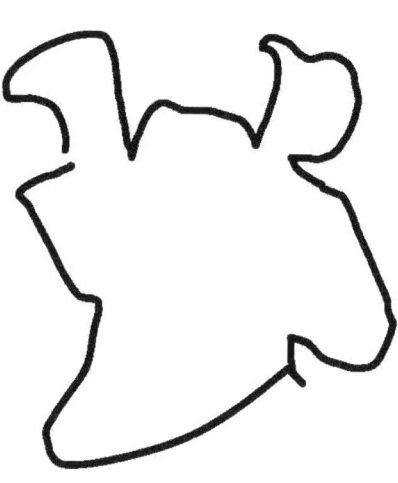

ON THE PATH

What does it take to overcome
Overcome the trauma of separation
Separation from those who love weus
Weus united we and us formed together
Together whether a short or long time
Time that is imbued with illusions
Illusions promoting close as frequent contact
Contact between we and us as that which unites
Unites the physical ignoring the spiritual
Spiritual requiring that higher level of connecting
Connecting all that we are beyond here
Here is not the only space required
Required to connect to both below and above
Above this world we find our reflection
Reflection of all our desires and joy
Joy that is without end only beginning
Beginning to integrate the here and now
Now is all there is as we take the journey
Journey to connect the disconnected
Disconnected ones are through lies traumatized
Traumatized by lies as they live through life
Life on the truth path is what it takes to overcome

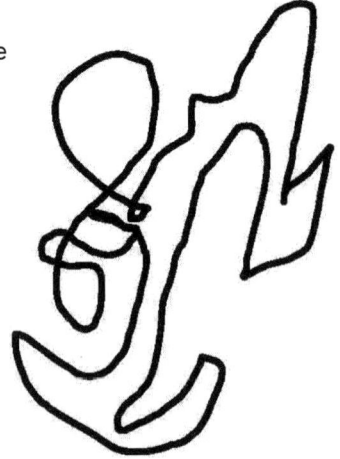

FIRST GREAT

Born of the first she is the first great
Great to be the one who will bring more
More than what we need one to satisfy
Satisfy our need for one to care and love
Love without doing more than just being
Being a beauty beyond compare the first
First to lead to the future of the family
Family built upon the past preparing
Preparing the way making it smooth
Smooth is the journey as well is now
Now we find within her reflection
Reflection of the inflection truly
Truly fulfilling the expectation until
Until reaching the level of maturity
Maturity now she is the first great

BURNING EMBERS OF HATE

Allowed the people to walk through
The burning embers of hate
Provided a way forward despite the
Searing heat burning through eons of racism
Showed the light at the end of the tunnel
Regardless of the darkness of nullification
Eased the distress of life's dangers
In the hands of the meaningless
Despite the barriers of barbwire
Concrete walls made a way of no way
What was untenable became possible
Knowledge necessary for truth
We have travelled the road evil
Seeking the good of people charged
Have used all our forgiveness overdone
To meet the forever in a harmonious space
This is the way of those seeking grace
Refusing to be the oppressors oppressor
Modeling those who walked through fire
Through the burning embers of hate

ONE PATH

Together we walk along one path
Path leading to where we go
Go to see that which is new
New to us in search of the all
All that is will be found internally
Internally is where exists the well
Well is both a place and a feeling
Feeling based upon the gifts
Gifts we are given in the before
Before we came to this place
Place when our vision dimmed
Dimmed when we turned from the light
Light of the world for us waiting
Waiting for the acknowledgement of now
Now is all there is on the way
Way to us on the holy journey
Journey together we walk along one path

CLOSING EYES

Closing my eyes I see your face
Face of beauty bringing delight
Delight springs within my soul
Soul bursting forth with joy
Joy beyond the limits of happiness
Happiness but for this regret
Regret of not listening to the Spirit
Spirit that provided the direction
Direction to the way complete
Complete was the union of us
Us is both you and me together
Together in our desire united
United in here and now then there
There is where we are complete
Complete in vision and voices
Voices shared until they are song
Song in harmony bringing image
Image of eyes closed I see your face

SPIRIT HELLO

Spirit to your spirit hello
Hello speak to me with song
Song of beauty and delight
Delight me with your sound
Sound in voice and in harmony
Harmony of mine and yours
Yours that brings delight to my soul
Soul which goes deeper than deep
Deep is beyond that which is seen
Seen only in the spirit world
World invisible to the eye but alive
Alive when we both open to its presence
Presence of a desire beyond waiting
Waiting to be with and a part of you
You who in the moment speak
Speak spirit to your Spirit hello

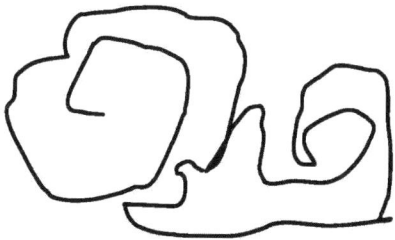

EASY DAYS

It was in the early days
Days where my imagination took flight
Flight from the now place of here
Here to then was such a short distance
Distance is the difference between now and then
Then was when I understood time
Time as an illusion falsified
Falsified by those who would control
Control the sense of our connection
Connection being the essence of life
Life as that which is required
Required as we journey from here to there
There as the false illusion of what was
Was at one time our sense that it passed
Passed from this memory to that memory
Memory as a whole event complete
Complete in our connections one to another
Another providing now to the early days

QUEEN IN GREEN

Please hear my pleading cry
As the queen in green passes by

See the queen in green
Beauty always a dream
Her silhouette flashes in the light
So amazing she turns day from night

See the lady in motion moving
Effortless movement body grooving
Her aroma jasmine like something new
Precedes her intoxicating not a few

See the queen in green
Beauty always a dream
Her silhouette flashes in the light
So amazing she turns day from night

Like the speaker losing lines
Unable in her presence to opine
From whence cometh she
To make one wish for thee

See the queen in green
Beauty always a dream
Her silhouette flashes in the light
So amazing she turns day from night

A beautiful sight a wonder
Lasting that spell all fall under

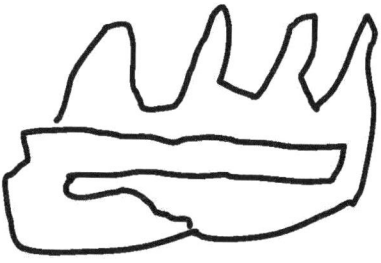

The dress of green float
Upon this sight one dotes

See the queen in green
Beauty always a dream
Her silhouette flashes in the light
So amazing she turns day from night

Come my queen to me connect
Willingly my all to you inspect
What can I do to you attract
A lowly beggar unable you to mack

See the queen in green
Beauty always a dream
Her silhouette flashes in the light
So amazing she turns day from night

Please hear my pleading cry
As the queen in green passes by

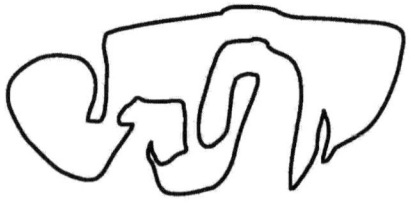

GREEN CAR

Today I was followed by a green car
Car seemed to have a driver beautiful
Beautiful to my eyes so alluring
Alluring enough spawning a desire to follow
Follow with my eye and spirit
Spirit led to this time and this place
Place where the car of green passed
Passed this scion of the spirit true
True to direct me in the way
Way to go on the path to connecting
Connecting to the beauty in motion
Motion so fast that the decision is now
Now is all there is and to succeed I must act
Act on the belief without information true
True to the dream world following two
Two of the same not different in kind
Kind that moved in alternate directions
Directions to follow one loved
Loved is the one in a green car

IN THE AIR

Up in the air many feet
Here the sky and clouds meet
I ride in comfort of my seat
Listening to the rhythmic drumbeat
There is where you I greet
In our loving moment we repeat

Down here on the ground
Places where we are around
The words shared us pure sound
Connecting one to another ever bound
It feels that within my heart you are found
Filling the complete space you abound

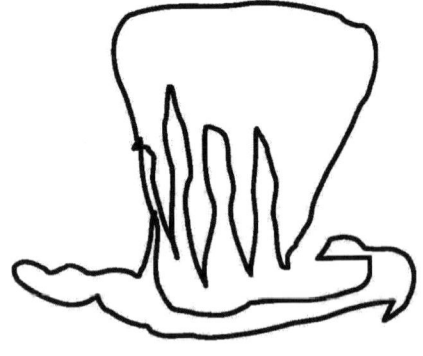

END OF BEGINNING

The end exists in the beginning
Beginning leads to the next steps
Steps and the incremental moments
Moments lead to minutes increasing
Increasing the time which is allocated
Allocated in the present to the future
Future is the expected desired outcome
Outcome results from investing time
Time is measured in their perception
Perception is in the present the all
All there is turns into knowledge
Knowledge grows from information
Information properly used is power
Power to overcome ignorance
Ignorance puts you at the mercy of tyrants
Tyrants glory in forming false opinions
Opinions that direct uninformed lives
Lives as they end exist in the beginning

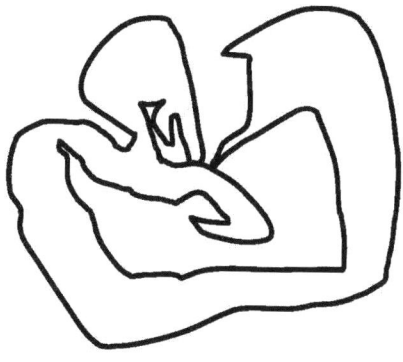

SHADOW

Shadow floated across the night
Night gave it an appearance of Black
Black as the night space without light
Light as the feather of Maat pure
Pure black speaking of truth
Truth in your heart confused by thought
Thought resting in the world of reality
Reality is a barrier to the true spirit
Spirit is the life within each being
Being as purity connects with the all
All there is can and will connect
Connect with the shadow understanding
Understanding I come to give gifts
Gifts of clarity with forever love
Love of the ancestor who watches
Watches you as the child of perfect
Perfect in the choices you make
Make your muse reflect the shadow
Shadow found across the night

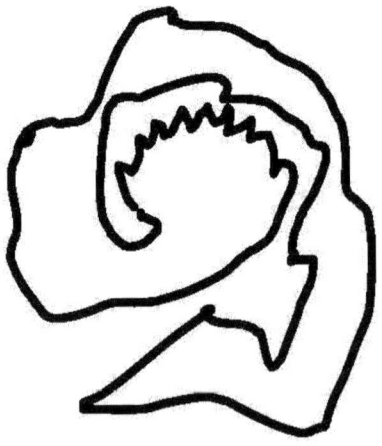

ONLY ONE

The desire to be one's only one
One is the joining of two combining
Combining the thoughts and feelings
Feelings reflecting this joining
Joining of the physical and spiritual
Spiritual is the essence of life
Life is reflected through in-loving
In-loving is the desire for living
Living is the outcome when connecting
Connecting of the stream of our thoughts
Thoughts that lead to truthful actions
Actions determine the way to knowing
Knowing what it means to find self
Self that understands is key found in purpose
Purpose as one's vision requires motivation
Motivation to unite with one significant develops holism
Holism recombines that which is different into same
Same leads to joining of two to one's only one

FADING DREAMS

Each moment my dream of weus is fading
Fading into the nothingness of lost
Lost is the memory of a mist
Mist is the description of not seeing
Seeing not clear is losing sight
Sight loss interfering with vision
Vision is dependent on goals
Goals are founded on the objectives
Objectives are the steps to now
Now is the only existence here
Here is where we can unite weus
Weus are the connective for our path
Path of in loving is replete with signs
Signs of how to join body and spirit
Spirit leads to the way perfect
Perfect is found within imperfection
Imperfection seems replete with opportunity
Opportunity is provided by the dream of weus is fading

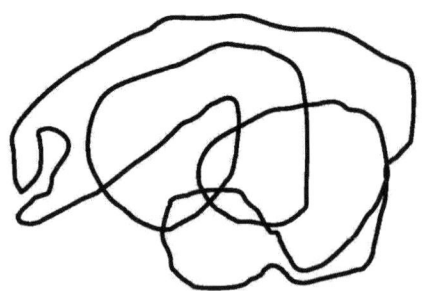

INSIGHT

Today I understand true sight
Sight is merely a portion of what
What it truly is 'tis a reflection
Reflection of what we call mist
Mist clouded the clarity of vision
Vision is created within the mind
Mind is the name we give creativity
Creativity is the ability to choose
Choose the limited to make unlimited
Unlimited is that we wish it to be
Be is always in the here and now
Now is all there is in our consciousness
Consciousness is to be aware of self
Self is the location of you within
Within the external is the internal
Internal is the location of insight
Insight makes clear true insight

SHOPPING

Those who think they are without go shopping
Shopping to find the value of what's missing
Missing is that which one thinks is better
Better than what is found in the now
Now is the only place where it exist
Exist in the location of both now and here
Here is what we are looking to obtain
Obtain the goods and services of desire
Desire leads one to seek what is missing
Missing is that which leads to fulfillment
Fulfillment satisfied that space empty
Empty is what one feels when incomplete
Incomplete is the sense of not being happy
Happy requires a unity of desire and acquiring
Acquiring is the movement to finding self
Self is the essence of getting too perfect
Perfect is to gain the all without shopping

FIRST AND LAST

To begin is the struggle to be first
First is an effort to avoid the last
Last is the position of those trailing
Trailing is to be behind the leaders
Leaders set the pace for the racers
Racers are those who attempt success
Success requires effort without recrimination
Recrimination lays the foundation for losers
Losers see the end as that which is difficult
Difficult is an idea that some may not be winners
Winners remove the mental obstacles
Obstacles that are created by the participants
Participants who win seek the goal using mindfulness
Mindfulness prepares the way for overcoming
Overcoming is the putting of plans into action
Action results when body and spirit are in motion
Motion of body and spirit allows us to be first

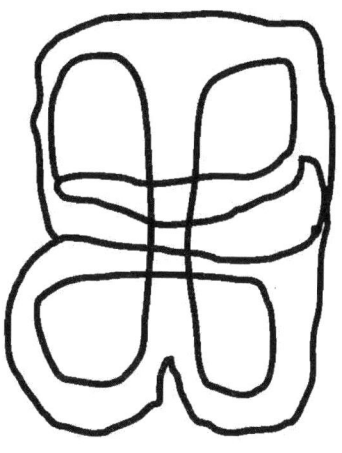

WHY HE CAME

Why did He come when he came
Came to remind the way for this people
People who thought it was enough to join
Join the organization that they defined
Defined them as separate and apart
Apart as the selected of their creation
Creation a process that they developed
Developed to set themselves apart and special
Special and chosen to be the one only
Only chosen and separate from the worldly
Worldly choosing the leaders as the way blind
Blind leading the blind needing new sight
Sight to show the way without a guide
Guide to aid the impaired to the way follow
Follow to the land of the way promised
Promised to meet the needs of the waiting
Waiting to understand why He came

WAITING

There is a place where you can sit and wait
Wait for the one who promised I will return
Return to be with you and take you home.
Home is where you can join together reconnecting
Reconnecting from the time that you have spent apart
Apart in the physical never apart within the spiritual
Spiritual connections are lasting and seen as eternal
Eternal is the way to focus when time is passing
Passing from one moment to the next as the clock moves
Moves from here to there it seems to go so slow
Slow is the way the waiting travel to the ending
Ending provide the way to accomplish time's termination
Termination of me is where you no longer have to sit and wait

CLOUDS

In the sky so blue there are many clouds
Clouds that seem to move while others still seem
Seem to be fluffy and white comprised of sunshine
Sunshine blocked by the ones that appear heavy and dark
Dark one the one that promises to bring rain down falling
Falling from the sky when the light blackens come together
Together waiting as one to blot out the sky blue
Blue that is high above the ones heavy or also without sight
Sight from above see them as the floor floating
Floating is if suspended in the air unattached
Unattached and not have any connection to the earth
Earth to sky in air filled there are many clouds

WRITTEN BY C. MICKEL

These lines are written by C. Mickel
C. Mickel wrote this verse following
Following the lead of the living son
Son of the father brother to brother
Brother now with the ancestors live
Live through a daughter and a grand
Grand bringing beauty and all joy
Joy that is lasting and increasing
Increasing the line through progeny
Progeny son and daughter name carry
Carry forth with pride and with grace
Grace through life and through love
Love expressed in connecting seed
Seed as genes promising living future
Future is assured through continuing name
Name will continue to be written by C. Mickel

BLACK BODY EXPERT

Not of color or knowledge am I an expert on Black bodies
Bodies that purport to so persevere pain
Pain acquired though the elevation of physical action
Action used to ensure that you and the masses are entertained
Entertained by your broken body or emotional exertion
Exertion to prove that what you choose to do is worthy of critique
Critique by an expert that has not the skill or courage to compete
Compete in the arena of those who are considered for their bodies unique
Unique bodies strong that resist openly pain and injury
Injury expected to not prevent the performance of skills to maximum level
Maximum performance is evaluated whether athlete is ill or well
Well is physical or emotional to the untrained uneducated eye
Eye that has not the discipline to determine the social or emotional state
State that is presumed to be whatever purports the limited expert
Expert simply because they have observed and written as an expert on
Black bodies

ACCEPTED CONTROL

Trading Black bodies for control of other Black bodies is accepted
Accepted is the right of those who control and are called owners
Owners are given the right to choose those who wish to be players
Players begin as volunteers who play without monetary rewards
Rewards may come in the form of the illusion of life preparation
Preparation for the sale of bodies to who would be their overseers
Overseers of what they do, how they look and what they are projecting
Projecting to the world that as rich people they have more choice
Choice to become enslaved to a system that has as its objective body control
Control of where the body goes, what the body does and how to deal with pain
Pain can only be controlled by proscribed means that are to owners acceptable
Acceptable as they are under the control of the owners and their supporters
Supporters that lay the foundation for the position control of Black bodies
is accepted

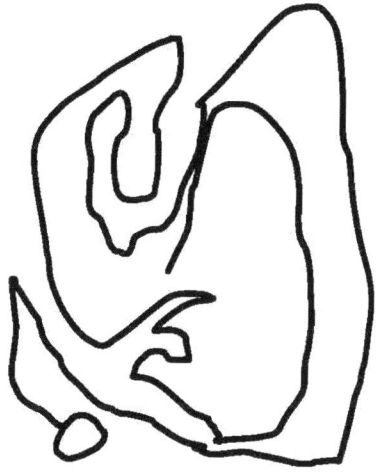

POSSIBLE

When lovers lose trust they then only believe in the possible
Possible is that which is based on the present physical
Physical evidence is that which can be held in the hand and mind
Mind what appears to be logical and consistent with the latest information
Information may not be the truth but has the appearance of one's truth
Truth is the perception of facts given by the senders to the receivers
Receivers structure the information as it fits into the narrative which is acceptable
Acceptable is formatted as what is socially constructed in communing
Communing is essential to formulation in the move from disconnecting
Disconnecting is the process resulting from all the physical to be paramount
Paramount is the choice made as some fail to invest in the alternative
Alternative to the physical is the quintessential essence that create life
Life exist physically or bears the spirit which allows belief in the possible

ANCESTORS

The life that we live in this world is influenced by ancestors
Ancestors play the role which leads to successful living when requested
Requested to be the intercessors they provide the information requites truth
Truth spoken to power providing the way for their descendants to travel
Travel in the moments when faced with crossroads of yea or nay
Nay to prevent movement outside of the structures of positive living
Living that meets the standards of the historic family of the way
Way to continue and reinforce the values of those who are conscious
Conscious that what is to be done is to improve and add value to the name
Name that reflects that these descendants are people who are worthy
Worthy of the sacrifices made by those who are now in the Spirit
Spirit directing those in the physical open to be influenced by ancestors

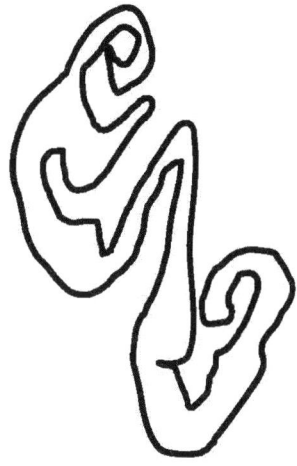

IGNORANCE

Ignorance is the key to understanding the physical/spiritual disconnection
Disconnection comes about through the loss of the ties that bind
Bind the continuation of the physical from the connected
Connected are those components which are essential to wholism
Wholism in the physical allows the development of the foundation for the spirit
Spirit is the higher level of the whole transformed with truthfulness
Truthfulness is the ability to overcome that which the confused accepted
Accepted is the understanding that can only be accomplished through truth
Truth is the way of Maat and overcomes the deleterious impact of Isfet
Isfet is the way of the disconnected as they make a way based on lying
Lying is the effort to avoid what is perceived as punishment based on fear
Fear is a preconceived notion that misinformation will prevent
physical/spiritual disconnection

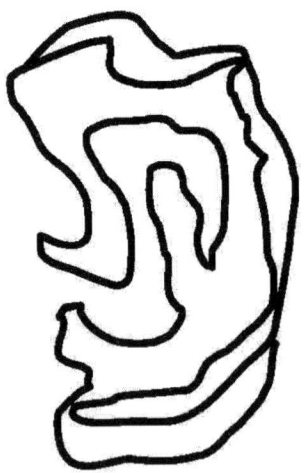

WISDOM

There is a road taken by a few based on the transformation of knowledge as wisdom
Wisdom takes information and changes it into that which is usable knowledge
Knowledge couched in the culture of those who would be successful
Successful users of these ideas can move from unknown to known
Known is based on the belief that what one professes is reality
Reality as a construct which provides the basis for acting on what is perception
Perception is comprised of knowledge as well as what the person values
Values are those components which undergird the desires as feelings
Feelings are expressed through the thinking process translated to emotions
Emotions seem to come from thin air but are a contribution to thoughts
Thoughts are reflective of the condition call imagination resulting in wisdom

HUSBAND OR WIFE

There are times when the husbands began to take the role or act like the wives
Wives may in some households have or be required to perform traditional roles
Roles that appear to be mis/male assigned or reserved for only the women
Women are it is proffered designed by their creator to be mates help
Help them to accomplish the task that have been assigned to their gender
Gender is viewed as related to the paternalistic roles assigned based on sex
Sex is the determinant of those who take the position that it is what is made
Made to see the world in a way that provides the path to your definition
Definition of what husbands are is related to how they are defined as they act like wives

ASKING WHY

There are moments where I question life's circumstances and ask why
Why am I feeling these feelings going through these emotions strong
Strong that flow in a manner painful knowing that I am here through choosing
Choosing to place my fate in the hands of connecting and reconnecting
Reconnecting with one who has in my heart betrayed the relationship again
Again and again due to the differing values and vision not choosing me alone
Alone choosing to satisfy their needs while maintaining an illusion of caring
Caring for one who cares for you secondary to the pleasure of options
Options that meet the needs at hand and not delaying gratification
Gratification through deceit while convincing oneself that this is honest
Honest is not outright misleading but not sharing the whole truth is not lying
Lying is relative to the specific question and not the answer that omits facts
Facts are clarification of questions and reveal the answer to and ask why

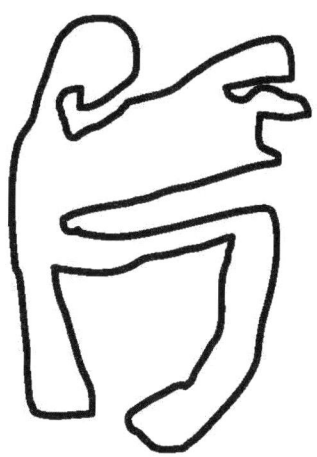

ALTARS

There is a place where those who appreciate ancestors build altars
Altars are sacred spaces here the descendants can choose to commune
Commune as progeny in the land of the living with those who are spirits
Spirits are purely the everlasting component of the living's energy
Energy that was not created nor can it be destroyed as it is eternal
Eternal is the life force that can be the voice that is heard from the dead living
Living in the sacred space but willing to provide earthly guidance
Guidance when the time is one of questioning and uncertainty
Uncertainty clarified defining the way when seeking the living go
Go to the place where we find the answers to the known and unknown
Unknown to the living can be clarified when seeking through ancestors
Ancestors are the resource that are always present and found as ances-
tors build altars

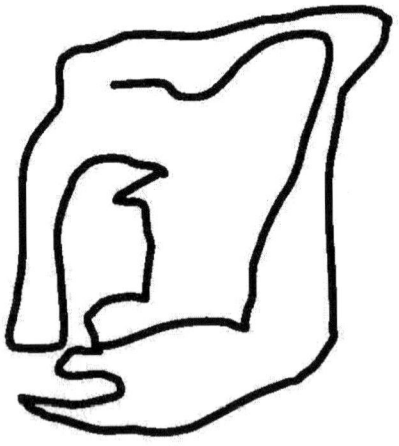

CAUSE/EFFECT

All actions result from a cause and end with effects
Effects are those following the cause resulting as consequences
Consequences do not appear without the decision of the actors
Actors are the instituters of behavior rather than recipients
Recipients began the process of effects and its concomitant causes
Causes thus began the process of happening turning into behaviors
Behaviors reflect the thinking and feeling of cause visible
Visible is the physical response of the effect that results
Results are the outcome of the instituting cause and end with effects

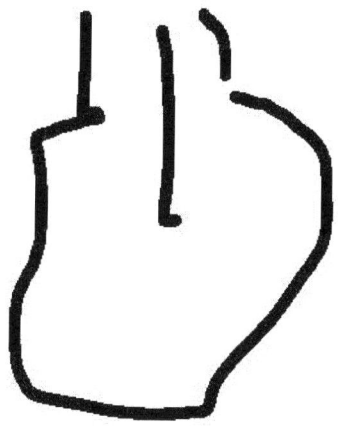

SOUL SUSTAINS

When one wishes to consume that which body and soul sustains
Sustains the entering process of the production of the cycle of living
Living is reflected in the birth growth, transition of each
Each life is reflective of the desire to be whole and complete
Complete is the outcome of the struggle to overcome that which whitens
Whitens is the substance which withdraws the life sustaining forces that
nourishes
Nourishes the seeds that fall from the living tree of all life
Life giving and growing with the deep roots firmly planted in soil
Soil rich from the nourishment of fertilizer we find which body and soul
sustains

TODAY

I remember you and me in all the days together especially today
Today is gone it is now the next day is now tomorrow
Tomorrow has come yesterday has faded it is here
Here is the precursor the next day a promised future
Future is the promised that if fulfilled provides the foundation
Foundation on which to build all that is yet to come into being
Being is the provision of the all which is required to exist
Exist together is the reality of being in the time called now
Now is all there is yesterday was tomorrow never comes all is especially
today

BRTHDY

These words are for my baby loved more than everyone
Everyone may call it the being born or birthday
Birthday is only for the unborn
Unborn is not a place or space for the created
Created can never be uncreated for eternity
Eternity is just that which is transformed
Transformed from one plane of existence
Existence is forever forth called
Called to reside on this plane if only a moment
Moment is that span of time equal to forever
Forever is where the spark of life resides
Resides in both thought as we it conceives
Conceives that we are part of the creator
Creator of all that exist including us
Us as a part that is never destroyed only changed
Changed is the limited which happens to physical self
Self is the visible manifestation of the changeless spirit
Spirit of the ever living created among us moving
Moving and living to the last day from the first
First life was also called being born or birthday

THESE LOVING HANDS

When I look at these hands there I find the sign of love
Love is what these hands were made to gently perform
Perform through the process of touching, holding, and caressing
Caressing those who are close as well is finding a way to contact
Contact who needs the touch that is physical as well as spirit touching
Touching is both in the present as well as in the future
Future is the gentle embrace and the loving connection
Connection not based on what is wanted but need fulfillment
Fulfillment based on truly loving not just for in the moments
Moments are instances of weus joined to connect the disconnected
Disconnected by selfishness and ownership of the relationship
Relationship is expressed though these loving hands where I find
Find the love you give as expressed through the sign of love

VESSEL OF LOVING

Love will always fit the vessel it is within
Within this container it will flourish
Flourish if it is provided the nourishment of light
Light to love is the return of the same feelings
Feelings reflected by the depth of each caring
Caring for me as I care for you is reflective
Reflective of the depth of joy shared therein
Therein exist the mixture of the lovers
Lovers give to their opposite vessel with trust
Trust that even in disagreement each is strong
Strong enough to withstand the adversity
Adversity is merely a blimp on life's radar
Radar which reflects the bond of unity
Unity and trust nourishes the unity of weus
Weus reaches out to provide complementarity
Complementarity means that which is in without
Without inside is reflected as face to mirror
Mirror of the expressions of loving are the vessel it is within

GEORGE TO GEORGE

Today we stand with Lloyd whose name is George
George reminiscent of another whose surname was Jackson
Jackson bothers dedicated to the liberation of African people
People who will never forget the sacrifice they made for freedom
Freedom of each of us which cost them their last full measure
Measure of blood and bone required of those who struggle without ceasing
Ceasing to be pleased by a little bit of life and require release
Release from the chains and shackles of the monster oppressors
Oppressors who would never release those in bondage without struggle
Struggle is the essence of the desire to be liberated without conditions
Conditions imposed require the chained to break the bonds asunder
Asunder is the act to shatter that which places the chains
Chains replaced by the beast that used the knee to debreath whose
name is George

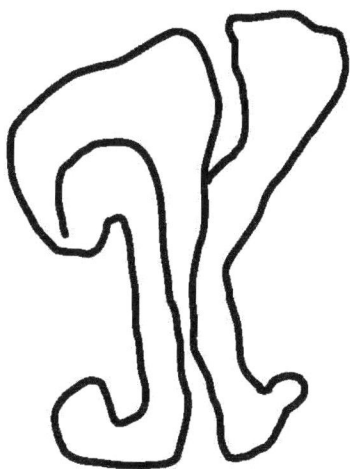

EVE

Traveling down the Nile sailing into the sun
Sun bearing down music playing Eve dancing
Dancing to the African bells and sounding drums
Drums beating to the movement of the lady beautiful
Beautiful is the swaying of the colors bright in the light
Light simmering off the river bouncing off African skin
Skin which reflects the love of life living lovely
Lovely is the night that gave birth to Eve a delight
Delight in your presence as we all travel the world together
Together we watch the morning break against the rim of the earth
Earth of green and blue, brown to dust releasing the moisture
Moisture that becomes the rain falling upon those walking
Walking from eve 'til morning sailing into the sun

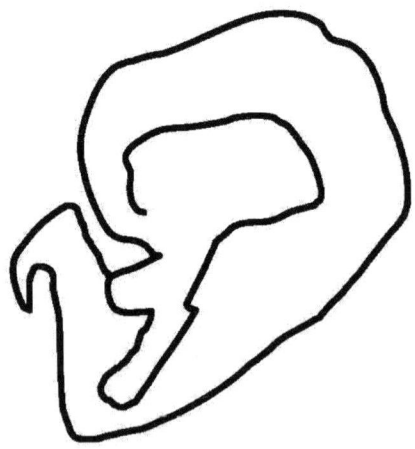

SOAP

Running water and liquid on a bar of soap
Soap that cleans away the dirt of lies and deceit
Deceit that infects the union of one to another
Another allowed to enter and make two clean a dirty three
Three to share the pristine connection breaking the bond
Bond based upon the ability of each to share all in unity
Unity of one resulting from two who commit to holding hands
Hands joined without any interference finger to fingers
Fingers intertwined unable to be broken by strong winds
Winds that blow push those united in the same direction
Direction uncertain but always together like bubbles on a bar of soap

SIGNIFICANT OTHER

No one accomplishes anything of worth without a significant other
Other that helps to lay the foundation for the altitude necessary
Necessary for the successful accomplishment of goals
Goals which lay the foundation for determining the foundation of success
Success is the joining of the separate one in the united two
Two is the very basic unit that is required in what is known as weus
Weus is the outcome of the selfish choosing to be united as unselfish
Unselfish is placing another in the position where they are the priority
Priority is the process of understanding at it is process of stepping back
to up stepping
Stepping up as the forerunner to providing the framework for the developing spirits
Spirits connected have few if any limits and are capable of all
All that ones becoming one are not found without a significant other

CONSTANT PRESENCE

To be in your constant presence is present of mine
Mine is the thought of you constantly
Constantly day and night awake or dreaming
Dreaming that we together journey through
Through all the ups and downs of this life
Life is so much richer with the union of two
Two who work well to bring about one
One out of the disconnected to be connected
Connected in both the physical and spiritual
Spiritual that represents the perfect
Perfect is that which expressed the corrected
Corrected in our thought and activities
Activities that bring weus closer
Closer than any other we fulfill expectations
Expectations to join one another in the path
Path between the things that are imperfect
Imperfect choices that bring about dis
Dis is the vision of that which is not wanted
Wanted is the correlation of a perfect present
Present is your constant presence is present of mine

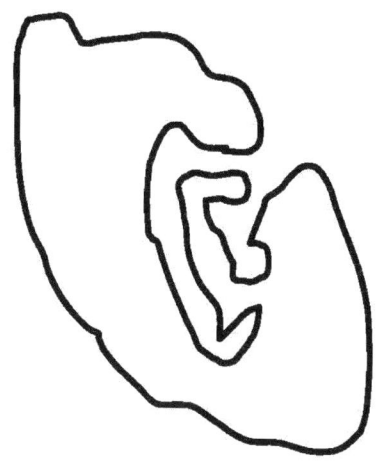

TOUCH OF DEATH

The kiss in the middle of the night awaking from a dream
Dream that the lips touched my cheek softly
Softly the lips brushed my face so lightly
Lightly but with such force from sleep awake
Awake with the fear of death a scream
Scream who touched me awaking from a dream with you
You me we are truth touched by this kiss of death
Death is only accepted if it leads to the transition
Transition of one to or of another is that which lives
Lives outside of the union of two
Two are so connected that me cannot exist without you
You awaken me the other life that is from a dream

I AM SO TIRED

I want you all to know I am so tired
Tired of reading about white people killing Black people
People who are trying to live in a world controlled by whites
Whites who use their belief in supremacy to oppress Blacks
Blacks who attempt to conform to their perceptions of right
Right is living not as the progenitors of human life
Life without the contribution of African people is less than full
Full of the many thousand gone who laid the foundation of today
Today but a veiled reflection of the Creator's desire
Desire that is written to be fruitful and multiply
Multiply the love of one another as time progressed from then to now
Now is the time to rise up and show the world we should
Should the oppressed act in a way to show the oppressor I am so tired

DARK

We the people of the dark
Dark is where we grew and became
Became that which provided the roots
Roots that connected our beginning to now
Now is the presence of our totality
Totality reflects the understanding clear
Clear is the vision within dark unseen
Unseen where the illusion of delusion
Delusion provided by controlled misinformation
Misinformation to lead those who are not informed
Informed that it is not the light leading
Leading to what makes part whole
Whole that developed in the dark right
Right that led the way contained light
Light is but a reflection of dark white
White is developed out of total blackness
Blackness was the original essence
Essence of life in process of developing
Developing in the face of the deep
Deep and lightless was this place
Place that is in its essence lightless
Lightless so pure that the amazed face
Face this we are people of the dark

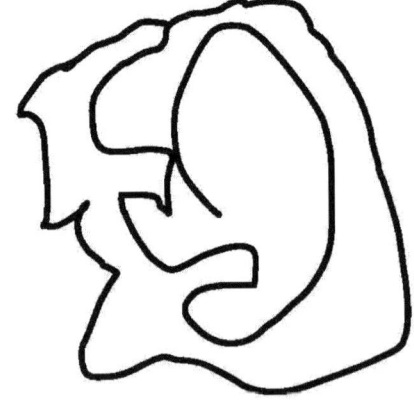

HAIL TO THE KING

The death of one born to struggle as the King
King refined through Benjamin Elijah without a crown
Crown of gold not required to be a leader
Leader revolutionary of millions by his words
Words of good trouble that provided the masses strength
Strength to take to the streets marching in opposition
Opposition to the gender race supremacy of some
Some who by maleness and the color of their skin rule
Rule the land promised from the beginning of the union
Union of the planter class only recognized we are men
Men born to be those who felt and acted superior
Superior to their women and those people of color
Color not white poor campaign considered unright
Unright needed to fight with hidden guns but nonviolently
Nonviolently acceptable to the oppressor became the cry of those
Those African soldiers on the way to war to Asians freedom abridge
Abridge by the militaristic system confronted by antiwar speech codified
Codified in the New York church rejected by many friends in the land
Land that purported to be promoting peace in the home of the brave
Brave was the King desiring to have a long life with those he led
Led to resist in Menefer betrayed by judas for those unjust
Unjust letter written leading to Lorraine a path to assassination
Assassination of the one born to struggle as a King

MASK

Each day I choose a mask to cover my face
Face that provides an explanation of feelings internal
Internal that reflect all that is known as well as unknown
Unknown is the appearance of the items used to cover the base
Base is the foundation for the covering of the reflection of eyes
Eyes that see a world that may be torn asunder by hate
Hate for those who reflect the light of the Dinknesh mother
Mother who laid the foundation connected the now to the beginnings
Beginnings which are the flower transported throughout the everywhere
Everywhere we behind the mask seek the way to join with love
Love of we united with us to form connection that is unbreakable
Unbreakable is the mirror that reflects the cover on my face

IT'S RAINING

Yesterday beauty into the world rain came
Came she to add joy to the family whole
Whole but incomplete without her presence
Presence bringing joy like love brought rain
Rain to nourish the ones who would her love
Love the space she filled with the promise of the future
Future bright is her smile laughing all the while
While she could a relative control who with love hold
Hold her in his arms taken by her charms
Charms as a blessing from blessing grew
Grew to the world one day she could master
Master in all the ways as beautiful could
Could be all she needed to be into the world rain came

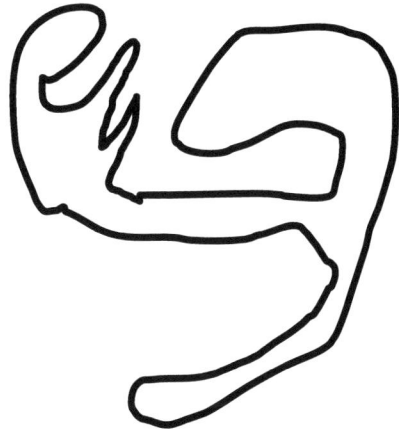

PLEASURE WITHOUT JOY

Our relationship is thoroughly pleasure without joy
Joy is the spiritual connected to the physical components
Components that excite the senses
Senses are those lone physical feelings
Feelings that give the illusion of completeness
Completeness is a false expectation of correction
Correction that occurs only with touch
Touch of my skin to your skin
Skin touching is where we find the sensation
Sensation that reflects the depth of lack
Lack of the invigoration of your presence
Presence that invigorates my imagination
Imagination of desiring your total goodness
Goodness of your good reflecting my desire
Desire transformed to lasting behavior
Behaviors leading to ways of connecting
Connecting intimately physical to spirit
Spirit is the quintessential road
Road filled with unsatisfying belonging
Belonging that is inconsistent pleasure without joy

I MET YOU

There was no we or us until I met you
You who are the muse a gift of creation
Creation which imbued our life
Life which you share as the creator
Creator of the beauty only you share
Share that which is acting and thought
Thought that it was shared with me alone
Alone I was spending my life sad
Sad that those who came soon left
Left with only the ideas of greater
Greater was the joining to come
Come together and see the sounds
Sounds taking us to creative heights
Heights that allowed us to hear colors
Colors of creation which laid the foundation
Foundation of sounds within love
Love of our union that cannot be broken
Broken by another only of ourselves
Ourselves who control the life essence
Essence of our direction together
Together and never alone as an individual
Individual where awaken until I met you

WHAT I THOUGHT

I thought I would die
I rolled the dice
Paid the price
Then lost my wife
I started to write
And my writing took flight
Then I thought that I would die
CJM

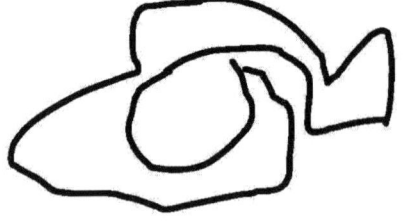

WORDS OF COLLEEN

ETERNITIES CORRIDOR

I have been here before
In the night where dreams
Take flight in eternities
Seeking him whom my
Soul adores.
Moments of lifetimes past tease
The mind and wet my face
Lord to my light appearing
Only in the night where
Dreams take flight in
Eternities corridor
Where do you go my beautiful one?
Tell me where you reside?
Is it only in the night
Where dreams take flight
In eternities corridor

Now you are here
My feet planted firmly on terra
My soul traveling a path
Through the spirit world
Seeking you lord to my light
My beautiful one whom my
Soul adores
Only known in eternities corridor

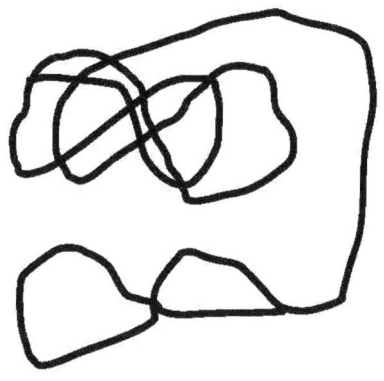

THANKFUL

To the self-existing one
Who gave life to all creation
Thank you
To the spirits providing
Guidance, giving light to darkness
Thank you
To ancestors who tread
The land long gone
Thank you
To creatures great and
Small for your vibrance
And resilience
Thank you
To family, friends, foes, and
Lovers who provided love and
Pain helping me to grow
Thank you
And to self so often forgotten
Who persevered through life's
Struggles never giving up and
Still became
Thank you

THANK YOU

These are the kindnesses that
Explain thank you
The deep wonder in your spirit
That capture my spirit bright
The quiet peace you leave in
The middle of the night
The explosive feelings you
Bring in the morning light
The time you take to speak of
The now we share
Your gentle approach the elicits
Liking causing me to care
The love in your heart our heart
My very being to dare
These are the words that
Require a thank you

BENDED KNEES

On bended knees with
Arms stretched wide I
Give thanks to the ancestors
Who unsparingly provide
Time stretches forth like endless night
No place to shelter for a heart without light
A gift very rare, a companion who share
The night was dark and my
Clouds hung low
But your caring like Ra's rising
Determine surviving early light shining
Early light warmed my
Heart like a lover's caress
Tenderly you soothed until
All was made well
The smile that you gave me
Shines in my face
Telling the world I am in a
Happy place
So on bended knees with
Arms stretched wide I
Give thanks to the ancestors
Who unsparingly provide you
Thanks

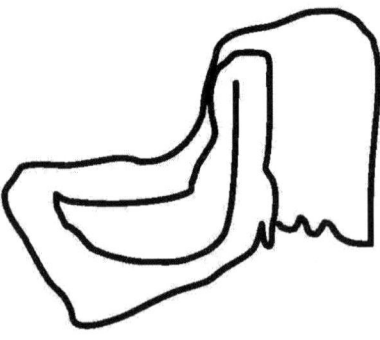

QUIETLY WE WAIT (for a friend's loss)

The pain is fresh
The hurt is new
Quietly we wait
Here to comfort you

A life barely begun. Now gone so soon
And parent's hopes, cast painfully strewn
Your heart filled with mourning
Your eyes filled with gloom
We stand by your side
To see through this wound
While quietly we wait, here to comfort you

There are no words or deeds to take away
this sorrow
to satisfy this pain we may only look forward
to tomorrow
A child received his angel wings
While heavenly being sing
And you are left to mourn
While quietly we wait, here to comfort you

SIMPLY MEANT TO BE

Simply meant to be two halves. but somehow whole, joined at the soul
We walk the trail of mystery only we two can see
Paths crossed worlds collided life force reconciled
No more separate I and me, instead only us and we face life's destiny
Simply meant to be

Simply meant to be joined at the soul two halves of a whole
Through spiritual eyes comes the ability to perceive
What was created now made perfect
Eyes shut tight
Third eye wide open
The beauty that is you flows freely
I drink you in
I breathe you out
The inevitable movement of what is life substance
Two halves now whole like puzzle pieces reconnected joined at the soul
Simply meant to be

Epilogue

What is written is to be written. The conclusion is just the beginning.
Confused hatred a year before to date lost my grand mother
A sense of frustrated loneliness
Wondering if God really loves me
My pride shamed annoyed I am in another storm
Surprised satisfied excited in awe the day my child was born
Disgust for those who give up anxious to live up surpassing all expectations
Jealousy nor envy I won't let it get me
Embarrassed feeling guilty the enemy is me
For gravity I show gratitude cause I can elevate escape and change my attitude
These words are dried blood on paper
They will survive when I'm with the creator
At times let it flow when I got the glow ain't one to gloat or boost or proclaim to be the Goat
Could been should've been would have been still can be him but that ain't my goal
Just another player in the play and we all got our roles
A Griot passing along parables

Christopher J. Mickel